GUITAR CHORDS
A FRETBOARD STICKER BOOK

GUITAR CHORDS
A FRETBOARD STICKER BOOK

HEREWARD KAYE

Thunder Bay
P·R·E·S·S
San Diego, CA

Thunder Bay Press
An imprint of Printers Row Publishing Group
10350 Barnes Canyon Road, Suite 100
San Diego, CA 92121
www.thunderbaybooks.com

© 2017 Quarto Publishing plc

All rights reserved. No part of this publication may be reproduced, distributed, or transmitted in any form or by any means, including photocopying, recording, or other electronic or mechanical methods, without the prior written permission of the publisher, except in the case of brief quotations embodied in critical reviews and certain other noncommercial uses permitted by copyright law.

Thunder Bay Press name is a registered trademark of Readerlink Distribution Services, LLC.

All notations of errors or omissions should be addressed to Thunder Bay Press, Editorial Department, at the above address. All other correspondence (author inquiries, permissions) concerning the content of this book should be addressed to Quintet Publishing at the address below.

This book was conceived, designed, and produced by
Quintet, an imprint of The Quarto Group

The Old Brewery
6 Blundell Street
London, N7 9BH
United Kingdom
T (0)20 7700 6700 F (0)20 7700 8066
www.QuartoKnows.com

QTT.CHORD

Thunder Bay Team:
Publisher: Peter Norton
Associate Publisher: Ana Parker
Publishing Team: April Farr, Kelly Larsen, Kathryn C. Dalby
Editorial Team: JoAnn Padgett, Melinda Allman, Traci Douglas

The Bright Press Team:
Managing Editor: **Rica Dearman**
Designer: **Paul Sloman** | +SUBTRACT
Photographer: **Neal Grundy**
Model: **Rory Indiana Kaye**
Senior Editor: **Caroline Elliker**
Associate Publisher: **Emma Bastow**
Publisher: **Mark Searle**

ISBN: 978-1-68412-080-2

Printed and bound in China

22 21 20 19 18 2 3 4 5 6

CONTENTS

Preface	6
Introduction	7
Level One: Trogg	18
Level Two: Quo	32
Level Three: Foo	48
Level Four: Zep	76
Level Five: Muse	128
Glossary	176
Index	178
Credits	180

PREFACE

I was nine years old when I heard my first electric guitar, a shiny red and white Fender Stratocaster. It was in the hands of Hank Marvin, lead guitarist of The Shadows, right up there on stage before me.

Hank's lead guitar lines were dripping in reverb. At the end of every phrase, his hand gently caressed the whammy bar, lending more beauty to the melodic moment. Beside him in perfect step, Bruce Welch on rhythm guitar was thrumming along to the urgent beat of the tom-toms behind. My eyes moved across to Jet Harris on the bass. He looked dangerous—like something loose, escaped from the lab!

Three guitarists paraded in front of me, one playing melodic jewels, one cementing the rhythm, one underpinning the sound on four fat bass strings.

We all remember our first time—but the second one's better! The next band I saw live on that same stage at the age of ten was The Beatles.

John Lennon was playing a Rickenbacker, belting out words like tortured metal. Across the stage, Paul McCartney was on his Hohner bass and George Harrison strummed a big, black Gretsch.

My eyes followed the leads from the guitars to the amps the band was plugged into: matching Vox AC30s (though Paul's bass amp was bigger)—dark, mysterious, and liveried in golden diamond thread.

I was totally inspired. Starry-eyed, I fell out of there and my baby heart was beating in 4/4 time and life had a soundtrack. I had to learn those Beatles' songs. I had to have a Vox AC30 (and all through my teens I did). I had to have an electric guitar!

In *Guitar Chords—A Fretboard Sticker Book*, I will take you on a similarly exciting journey of your own, which will help you learn how to play the guitar as quickly as possible. We'll start with an introduction to the basic elements, and I will show you how to play a variety of chords. You can use the colored stickers at the back of the book to help you remember these, and the more advanced chords, scales, and guitar tabs that you'll learn as you move through each level. Follow the simple instructions, and you'll be playing the guitar in no time!

Hereward Kaye

INTRODUCTION:

A few basics before we start, including anatomy of the guitar, how to hold, pick, or strum it, and how to name your strings. Also, a guide to what lies ahead in this book, with an explanation of the fingerboard diagrams you will encounter, and how to use the stickers.

INTRODUCTION

This book is dedicated to getting you playing guitar as swiftly as possible, traveling through all the chords from A to G, where A = Absolute beginner, and G = Guitarist!

It all begins with one simple chord: A minor. This is your fast car that will whizz you northward from bewildering darkness to enlightenment. It only takes a few chords and a bit of strumming technique to be able to play literally hundreds and thousands of songs. Your journey through those first chords could not be more simple. They will be arranged in such a way that you only need to move a finger, sometimes two, to get from one to the other.

As you progress through this book there will be many more chords, but don't let them frighten you. Just start at the beginning, follow the instructions with the help of our color-coded stickers, and Bob (Marley, Segar, Dylan, Weir) will be your uncle!

There'll be diversions along the way: basic strumming, fingerpicking, and how to count time, some essential music theory, but all stripped down to the basics and arranged in such a simple way that we get you playing for your own pleasure in double-quick time. That is our mission—and your journey.

ROAD MAP (HOW TO USE THIS BOOK)

Each chapter aims higher than the one before and can be referred to individually, depending on your skillset from the outset. So the chapters are presented here as levels. Are you a rudimentary Trogg? Or a beginning-to-get-it-together Quo? Are you a really not-too-bad Foo? Or a "now that's what I call music" Zep? Whichever you are, aspire to be a Muse! I mean, who would not want to?

A NOTE TO LEFT-HANDERS

Although the photo illustrations and fingerboard diagrams are all in the right-handed guitarist position, the fret and finger positions are **exactly the same** for a left-handed player, **providing** you are playing a left-handed guitar, appropriately strung. Just follow where we show you to put each finger on the frets, and you will be able to use this book perfectly.

THE **STICKERS**

Peel the reusable sticker away from the backing and insert it under the string wherever indicated. Don't sticker more than three chords at a time on your fretboard or it will get too busy.

In the early stages of this book we will give clear instructions for which stickers to use, until you get used to the system.

HOW TO **HOLD A GUITAR**

- Sit down to learn, on a stool or chair without arms.
- Sit up straight. Don't lean back lazily or the guitar will spoon outward in your lap and make it difficult to bend your left hand round to the fretboard.
- Adjust the strap so that it helps support the guitar, with the curve resting on your knee. Make sure you're sitting comfortably.

HOW TO **HOLD A PICK**

- Hold the wide part of the pick or plectrum (same thing!) between thumb and forefinger.
- Don't grip it too tight.
- Don't hold it too far down. Leave half of it showing, to connect with the string.
- Don't hold it too slack or the string will knock it from your fingers.

INTRODUCTION

NAME YOUR **FINGERS**

- **Right-handed players:** hold your left hand up in front of your face. This is your "fretting hand" that will shape your chords.

- **Left-handed players:** hold your right hand up in front of your face. This is your "fretting hand."

- Finger number 1 is next to your thumb.

- Finger number 2 is your middle finger.

- Finger number 3 is next to your little finger.

- Your little finger is finger number 4.

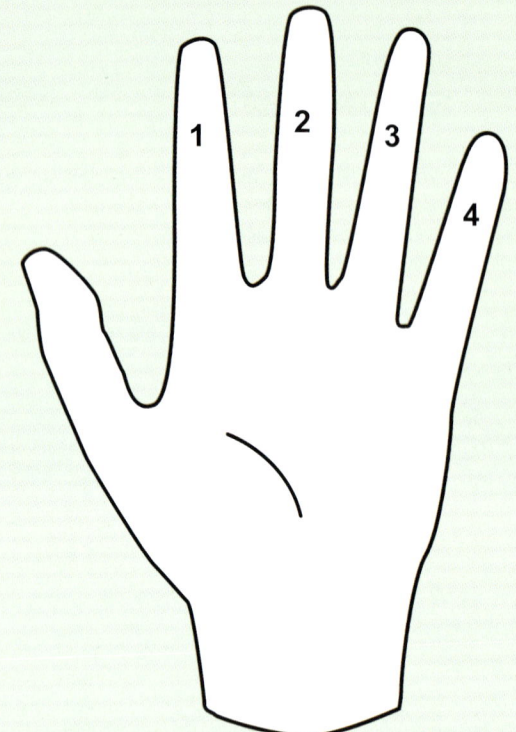

FINGERBOARD **DIAGRAM**

Next to each photo of the chord in action is a fingerboard diagram. You can see that the grid is a picture of the first four frets (fret numbers shown in Roman numerals) and the six strings of your guitar (the horizontal lines), assuming the nut is at the right, and the name of each string. A number on a string within two fret bars shows you which finger to use and where. A small x just to the right of the nut will denote whenever a string is not to be strummed with that particular chord. A small o denotes whenever a string is to be left open—strummed, but no finger on the string.

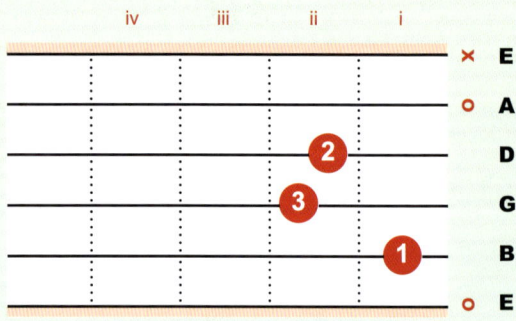

ONE CHORD LEADS **TO ANOTHER**

The chords in this book will not immediately be presented to you according to their key of A, B, C, D, E, or G. Neither will they be arranged according to their "family group" or type (i.e., Major, minor, dominant 7th, Major 7th, etc.).

As our mission is to get you playing as directly as possible, the chords early in this book are organized in terms of **which chord leads most easily to the next one**. As the book progresses, you will again come across these chords—and many more—organized into distinct family groups.

SHARPS AND **FLATS**

You may notice that the same notes and chords are sometimes referred to as sharps and sometimes as flats. The note in between A and B, for example, is referred to as both A sharp and B flat. This is because it is **sharp of A (i.e., above) and flat of B (i.e., below)**.

When a chord is a sharp it will be indicated by #. Think of sharp as meaning "higher." When a chord is a flat, it will be indicated by ♭. Think of flat as meaning "lower." Sharps and flats can be very confusing to the musical beginner, particularly as chords have a "sharp" name or a "flat" name, depending on the key that you're in. In this book, chords will be referred to as sharps when we are traveling up the fretboard (toward the body of the guitar), and flats whenever we are traveling down the fretboard (toward the headstock).

Don't worry too much about these when you first start out—you'll learn more about them as you progress.

PICKING UP, **ALONG THE WAY**

As well as plenty of chords, there's other stuff you need to pick up along the way. How to **tune your guitar** and how to **change a string**—think of it like car maintenance!

We will teach you to strum, count time, and perform a basic fingerpick. You'll learn how to read a **tab** and find tips on **technique**—hammer-ons, slides, and bends, etc.

And, although we don't encumber you with musical notation here, necessary basic **theory** is gradually introduced, and we include a few **scales** (Major, minor, pentatonic, and blues scale). This book will also teach you how to **improvise**.

INTRODUCTION

ANATOMY OF A **GUITAR**

Whether electric or acoustic, your guitar is made up of headstock, neck, and body.

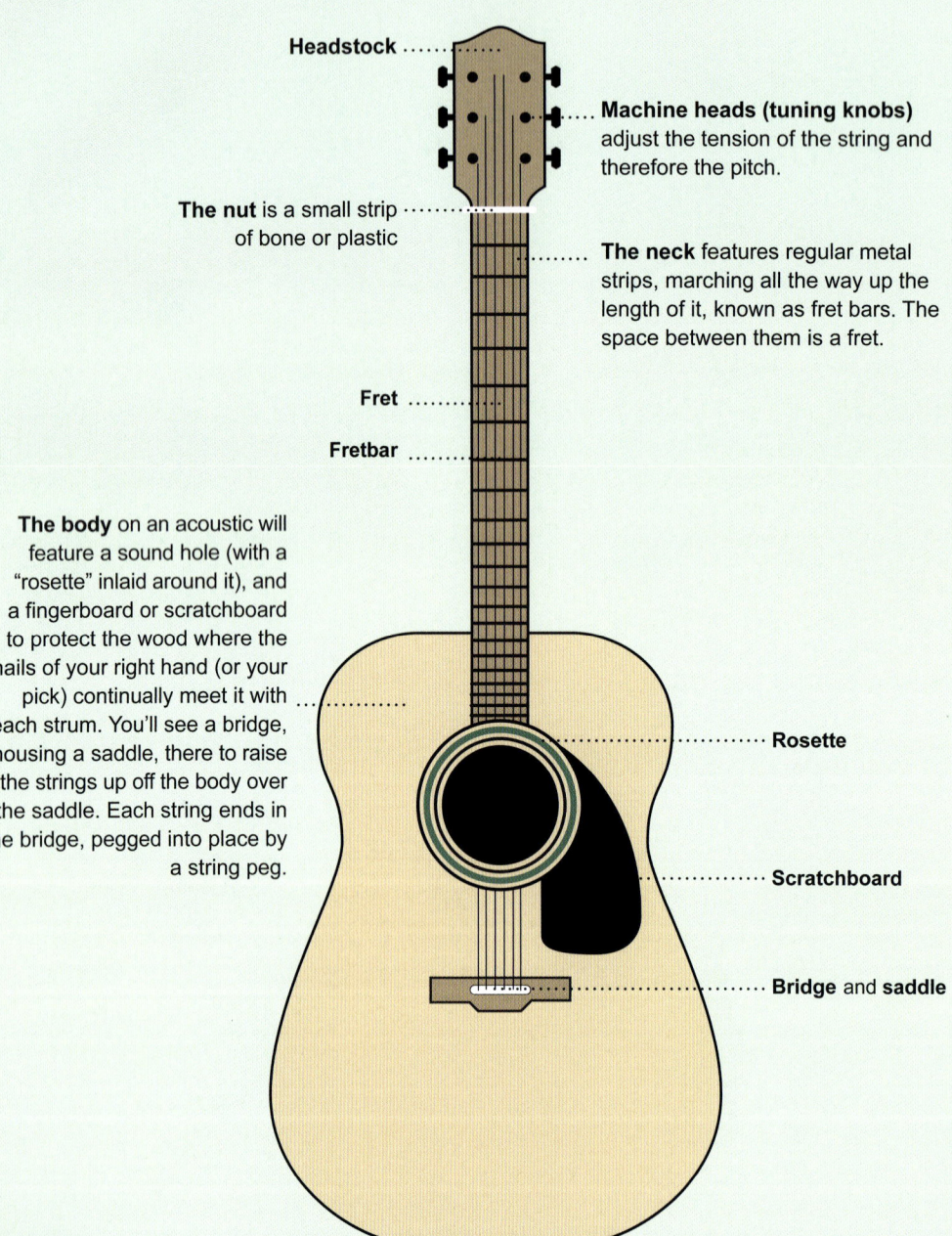

Headstock

Machine heads (tuning knobs) adjust the tension of the string and therefore the pitch.

The nut is a small strip of bone or plastic

The neck features regular metal strips, marching all the way up the length of it, known as fret bars. The space between them is a fret.

Fret

Fretbar

The body on an acoustic will feature a sound hole (with a "rosette" inlaid around it), and a fingerboard or scratchboard to protect the wood where the nails of your right hand (or your pick) continually meet it with each strum. You'll see a bridge, housing a saddle, there to raise the strings up off the body over the saddle. Each string ends in the bridge, pegged into place by a string peg.

Rosette

Scratchboard

Bridge and **saddle**

ELECTRIC

The body on an electric has much more going on. There are pick-ups, which do exactly that—pick up the sound and relay it to the amplifier. A pick-up switch allows you to use the pick-ups in different combinations, thus varying the tone. Tone control knobs allow you to make further adjustments from bassy to trebly—bottom or top, in muso-speak. Just experiment. Use your ears, trust your ears, find a sound you like. Some electric guitars also contain a whammy bar—a tremolo arm that wobbles the bridge around and allows you to "portmento" the pitch of the strings up or down. You'll also find a jack input socket, into which you plug in your lead.

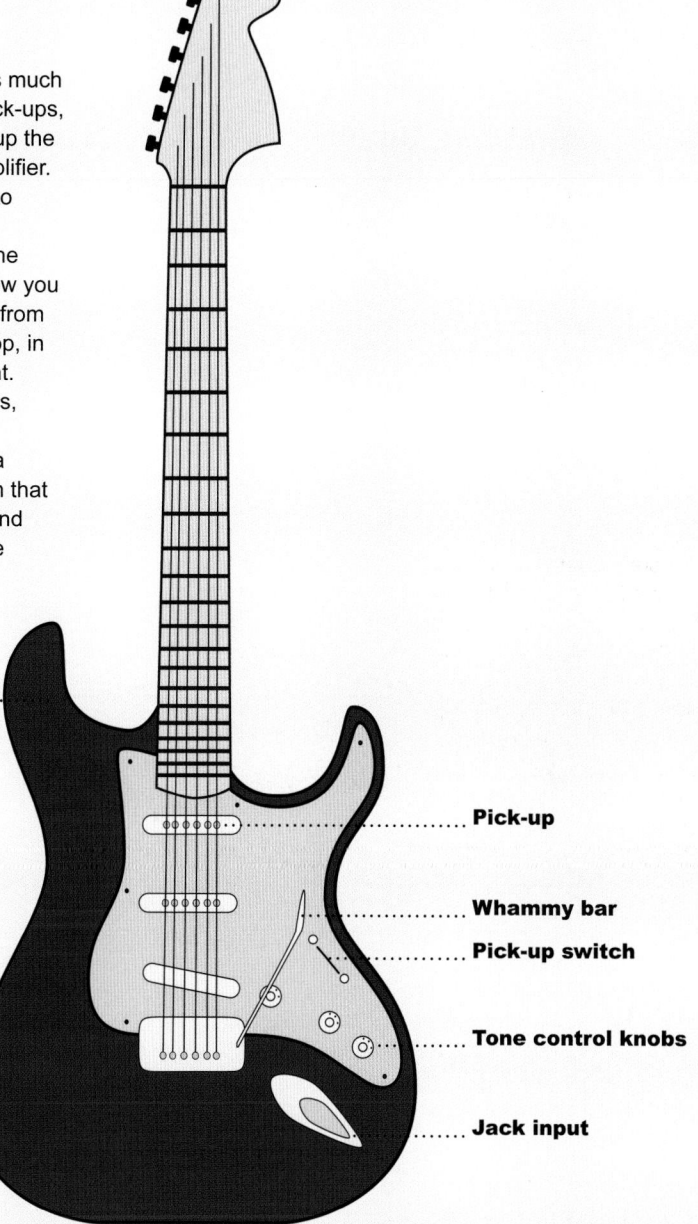

Pick-up

Whammy bar

Pick-up switch

Tone control knobs

Jack input

INTRODUCTION

A GUIDE TO THE **STRINGS**

Remember their names from the thickest—bottom E, the lowest in pitch, situated at the top of your fingerboard diagram—to the thinnest—top E, the highest in pitch, situated at the bottom of the diagram.

They are:

E^{6th} A^{5th} D^{4th} G^{3rd} B^{2nd} E^{1st}

Here's a much easier way to remember them:

Eddie   **A**te   **D**ynamite   **G**ood   **B**ye   **E**ddie!

Pluck each string, from lowest to highest—in other words, thickest to thinnest. As you do, name it out loud.

Test yourself: pluck a string at random and name it.

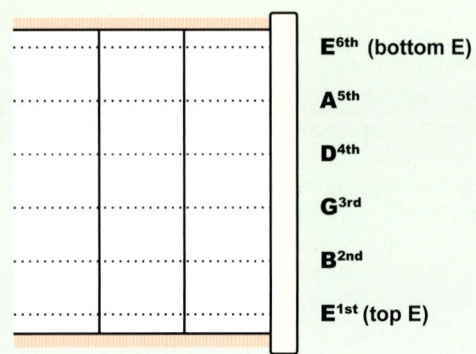

E^{6th} (bottom E)

A^{5th}

D^{4th}

G^{3rd}

B^{2nd}

E^{1st} (top E)

FRETTING HAND

Allow your thumb to move freely at the back of the neck and go wherever most helps the particular chord you are shaping on the fretboard. Don't allow your thumb to grip too hard or it will start to ache. Keep the nails on your fretting hand cut short so you can bear down on the strings with your fingertips, and keep your knuckles in the air. When you strum, press down hard to allow the notes to really ring out. It will hurt at first, but your fingertips will toughen with practice.

STRUMMING HAND

Keep your wrist flexible to allow for a relaxed and fluid strumming motion. While the fretting hand is required to press down fiercely on the fretboard to produce a clear note, your strumming hand should be much more gentle and graceful in approach. Don't smash down on the strings—let the amp do the work.

A GUIDE TO **THE FRETS**

The first space (between the nut and the first fret bar) is fret 1, the next one up fret 2, and so on. Press down hard on a string in the space between two fret bars (never on the fret bar itself, which produces a nasty buzzing sound) and pluck that string. Then, move up to the next fret and do the same. You'll hear the pitch of the note is now higher. It has gone up exactly a semitone; one half-step on the chromatic scale.

Now notice the inlay on the fretboard—usually white dots—situated in the third fret up from the nut, then the fifth, the seventh, and ninth (if not located in the fret, they will be running along the side of the neck). Now look at the twelfth fret. Two dots. These dots are markers to help you get your bearings. The double-dots on fret number 12 mean you are now a full octave up from the open string. Try it! You can hear it's the same note when pressed as when open, albeit pitched an octave higher.

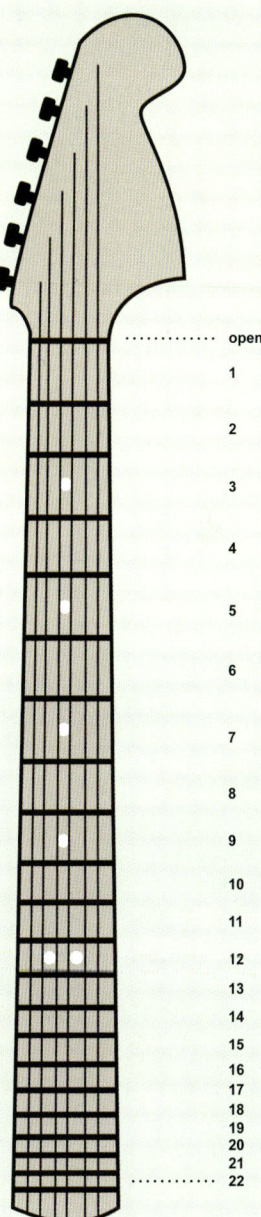

INTRODUCTION

STRUMMING

Playing guitar is a two-handed affair. Whether left-handed or right, our stronger hand strums and our weaker one forms the chords. And we pull all our focus onto the hand forming the chords, putting our fingers on all the right places and being highly disciplined in attention to detail with our fretting hand.

But I would say, with your strumming arm—let yourself go! Feel the rhythm and express yourself—free your mind, feel the groove, set your strumming arm free.

There are techniques, of course. There will be basics to be mastered as you progress through the levels of this book, but it's simpler than you may think.

- Keep your elbow back and keep your wrist flexible to allow for a relaxed and fluid strumming motion. (Be nice and "wristy," like a good tennis player.)
- Keep your hand close to the strings so that you're never having to travel far to get back to the next strum.
- Use downstrokes and upstrokes (we'll show you how).
- While the fretting hand must press down fiercely on the fretboard to produce a clear note, your strumming hand needs to be much more gentle and graceful in approach. Remember, don't smash down on the strings—let the amp do the work!
- Bring the palm of your strumming hand down on the strings when you don't want them to sound (this is called a "palm mute").
- Plug your musical self into the groove of the song you're playing along to and striving to mimic. Feel that rhythm, give it a go! We all feel the music and move to it in our own individual way. Allow your strumming hand to do exactly that.

HOW TO USE **THE STICKERS**

In the early days of chord learning, the stickers will be key to formatting your position on each chord. We recommend that you do not sticker more than three chords at a time, or your fretboard will become too busy.

When marking up more than one chord at a time, you may find two different finger positions vying for space on the same fret position. Don't worry. There's room on the fret to accommodate two stickers side by side, or even slightly overlapping.

You will discover that this book is about more than chords, as you come across single-note sequences, such as riffs and scales. You'll be at a level where you may not need the stickers to memorize a three-chord sequence by then. But for marking up the eight notes of the chromatic scale, for example, they could be invaluable!

STEP-BY-STEP

Take a look at the example chords below. Three chords are stickered, and you will be playing them in sequence, moving from one color to another.

- Two chords share the same finger position. The stickers are small enough to sit side by side.

- To place them, drop them on the fretboard, and use a fingernail to nudge them into place under the string.

- Press down firmly on the string over the sticker to secure it.

- When you want to remove the stickers, simply ping them off using your fingernail or your pick. The adhesive is gentle enough to leave no residue.

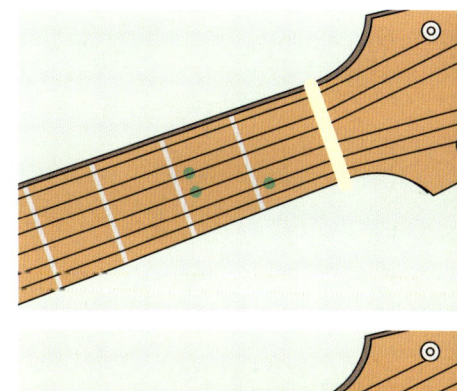

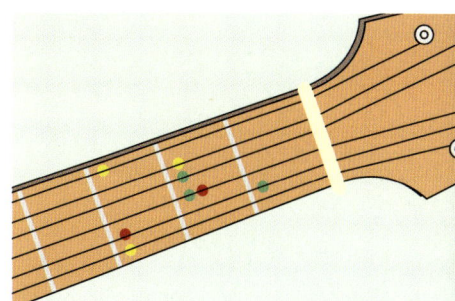

GOOD TO GO

Refer to the glossary at the back for a definition of all the technical terms used in this book.

LEVEL ONE: TROGG

At this first level, we'll teach you how to count basic time and play your first ten chords. We'll also show you how to use a capo, tune your guitar, and change a string.

When the Troggs started out, their sound was labeled "Caveman Rock," which is appropriate—you haven't learned to talk guitar yet!

Left: British band The Troggs had major hits during the 1960s

LEVEL ONE

COUNTING TIME: 4/4 QUARTER BEATS

We can all count, but this is counting the beats of a bar and it's vital. All music is divided up into bars. Each bar is divided up into beats. As a fledgling musician, you need to be counting the beats constantly in your mind, until you don't need to anymore. Count this aloud, at an even pace: 1, 2, 3, 4. Each of these beats is a quarter of a bar (in musical notation, one crotchet).

STRUMMING: ONE IN THE BAR

Now, remembering your count of 1, 2, 3, 4, you are going to count yourself in for one bar, then strum the open strings on the first beat of the next bar, like this:

(count) 1, 2, 3, 4—strum, 2, 3, 4

Nice one. What you need now is a chord!

YOUR FIRST TEN CHORDS

You are about to learn one chord that will lead you almost immediately to nine more! We're going to do it in five short sequences. Use the accompanying photos, fingerboard diagrams, and stickers to guide you through. Once you have mastered each short group of chords, strum them one in the bar, counting aloud.

A minor

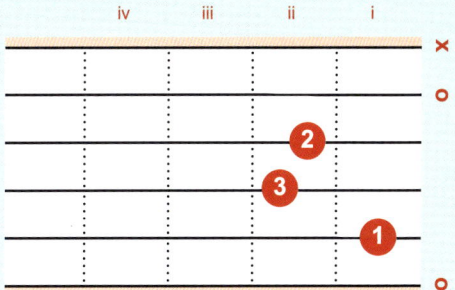 

This is **A minor** (referred to as **A**^m).

- Finger 1 goes on the B string on fret 1.
- Finger 2 goes on the D string on fret 2.
- Finger 3 goes on the G string on fret 2.

An **x** beside E^{6th} (at the top of diagram) tells you not to strum this string, so you will be starting the strum from the A string immediately below it.

A small **o** beside E^{1st} (at the bottom of the diagram) tells you to strum this string, even though you have no finger on it. The **o** denotes open.

Now, assign a sticker color to this chord, say, red. Mark it up on your fretboard, using the removable red stickers in this book.

LEVEL ONE

Your next chord is an **E Major** (referred to as **E**). It's the perfect next chord to learn, because it's exactly the same shape, just one string higher up!

So, from A minor, try and maintain the same hand shape, just move it in an upward direction (toward the ceiling) one string.

E Major

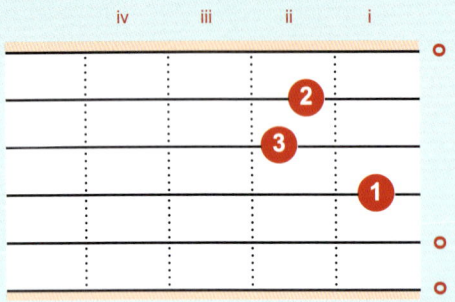

- Finger 1 goes on the G string on fret 1.
- Finger 2 goes on the A string on fret 2.
- Finger 3 goes on the D string on fret 2.

Start the strum from E^{6th} and strum all the strings. Assign a sticker color to this chord, say, green. Mark it up on your fretboard using the removable green stickers at the back of this book.

WHAT'S A CAPO?

A capo's function is to raise the pitch of all the strings equally and simultaneously, allowing you to play in a variety of keys. It clamps tightly over any fret. From there, play all your chords in exactly the same way you are used to. You'll hear that it brings a whole new color to them. It's a great tool if you're a songwriter, and particularly useful if you're a singer/guitarist. If a song you've just learned from a track is in the wrong key for your voice, try the capo across different frets until you find the key that suits you.

Your next chord is an **E minor** (referred to as **Eᵐ**). From E Major, simply remove finger 1. Voila, E minor! No need to "sticker" this one. Strum all the strings.

E minor

CHORD SEQUENCE: Aᵐ - E - Eᵐ

You are now going to play those three chords in sequence. Count yourself in: 1, 2, 3, 4, then strum the chord on the first beat of the next bar, like this:

(count) 1, 2, 3, 4—strum, 2, 3, 4, and so on.

1	2	3	4		1	2	3	4		1	2	3	4		1	2	3	4
Count				-	Aᵐ				-	E				-	Eᵐ			

23

LEVEL ONE

A minor 7th

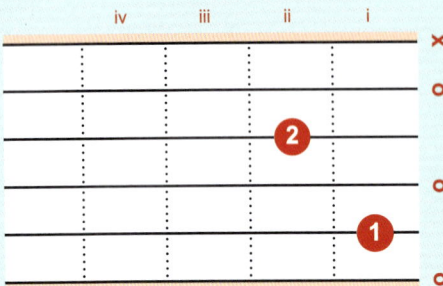
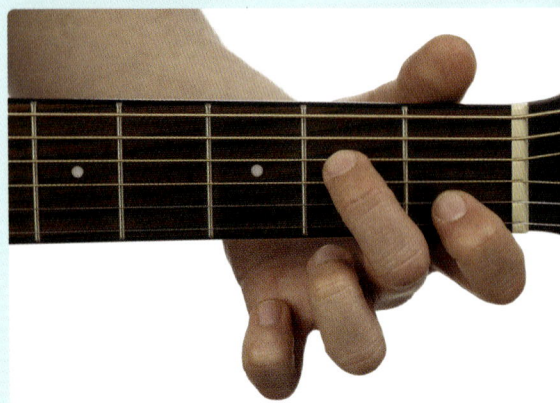

For **A minor 7th** (referred to as **A^(m7)**), play an A^m and remove finger 3.

E dominant 7th

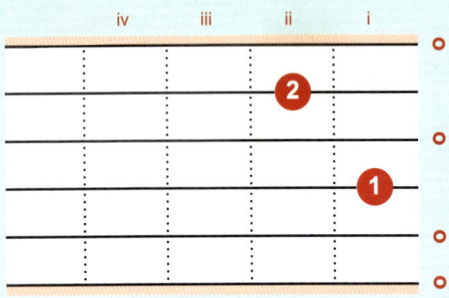
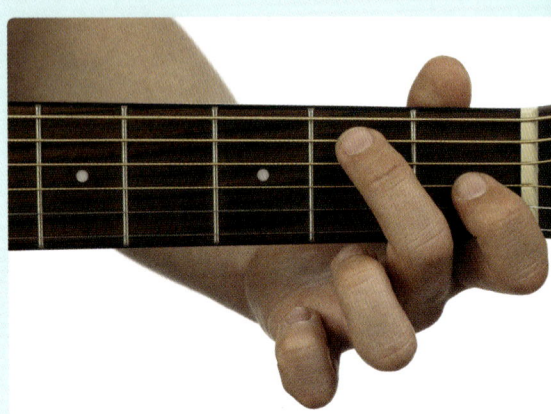

For **E dominant 7th** (referred to as **E^7**), play an E and remove finger 3.

CHORD SEQUENCE: A^m - A^(m7) - E - E^7

Count yourself in: 1, 2, 3, 4, then strum the chord on the first beat of the next bar, as before:

1	2	3	4	1	2	3	4	1	2	3	4	1	2	3	4
A^m				-	A^(m7)				-	E				-	E^7			

C Major

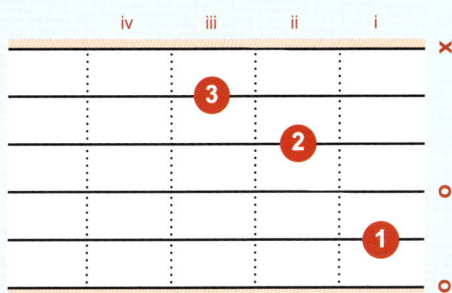

To play **C Major** (referred to as **C**), go back to your first chord of A^m (probably still stickered in red). Now lift finger 3 and move it to A3—i.e., the A string, third fret.

C Major 7th

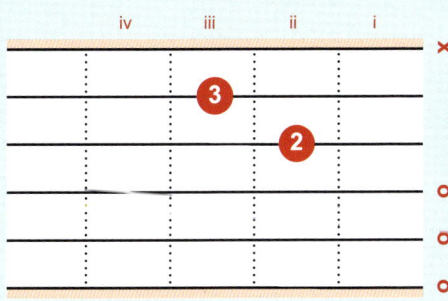
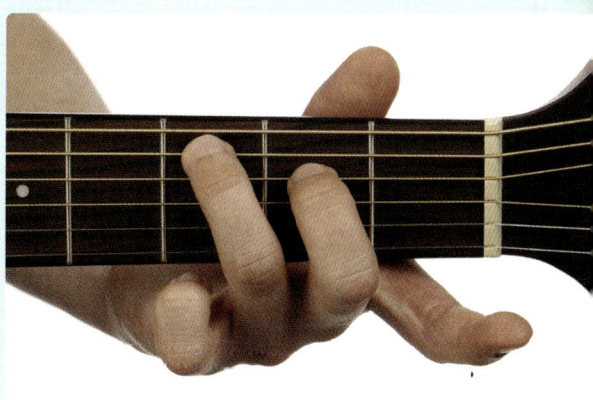

To play **C Major 7th** (written as **C△**) from your chord of C, simply remove finger 1.

CHORD SEQUENCE: A^m - C - C△ - C

A small triangle beside the C denotes the Major 7th. Count yourself in: 1, 2, 3, 4, then strum the chord on the first beat of the next bar, as before:

1	2	3	4	1	2	3	4	1	2	3	4	1	2	3	4
A^m			-	C			-	C△			-	C			

LEVEL ONE

Your next chord is **G Major 6th**, or **G⁶**.

G Major 6th

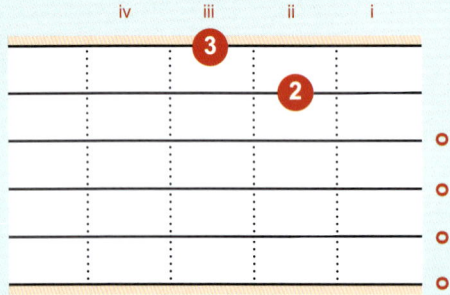

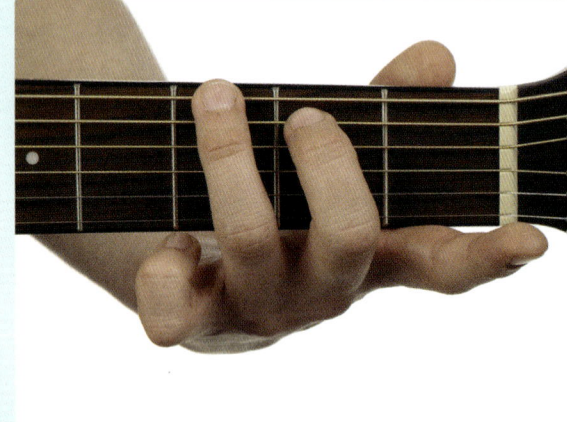

To play **G⁶**, first go back to your chord of C Major 7th and just move it in an upward direction (toward the ceiling) by one string. Assign a new sticker color to the chord of G⁶—yellow. Mark it up on your fretboard, using the removable yellow stickers in this book.

Do you still have the chords of A minor and E Major stickered on your fretboard? If you do, you'll notice you need to put a yellow sticker beside a green one, because G⁶ and E Major are vying for the same spot, in the finger 2 position (A string, second fret).

G dominant 7th

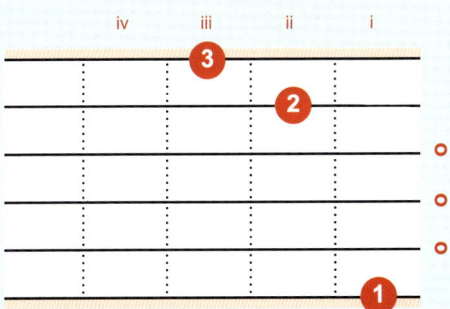
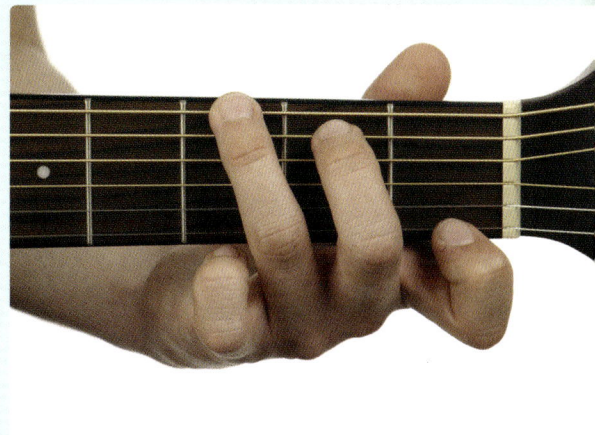

From G^6 just add finger 1 on fret 1 and you've got G^7.

You already have three chords stickered, so I would recommend you just commit this last one to memory!

CHORD SEQUENCE: C - C$^\triangle$ - G^6 - G^7

Count yourself in: 1, 2, 3, 4, then strum the chord on the first beat of the next bar:

1	2	3	4	1	2	3	4	1	2	3	4	1	2	3	4
C			-	C$^\triangle$			-	G^6			-	G^7			

LEVEL ONE

CHANGING YOUR STRINGS

Whenever they begin to sound dull, change your strings—there's nothing better or more professional than the sparkling bright sound of shiny new ones. To do the job properly, in addition to an appropriate set of strings (ask in the store), you will need a guitar tuner, peg-winder, and wire cutters.

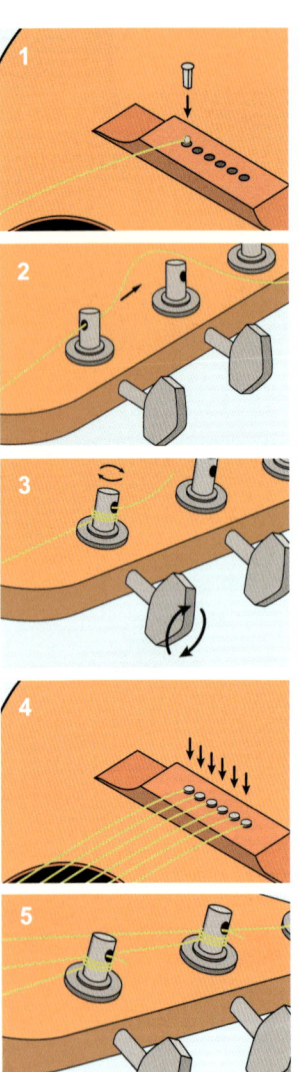

Follow these steps to change your strings:

Slacken all your old strings, then cut through them one at a time with your wire cutters, unthread from the machine head, and dispose of.

You now have the other six halves of your strings protruding from the bridge. If your guitar is an acoustic, the peg-winder has a U-shaped hole cut out of the end, for prising the gromits out of the bridge. If it's an electric, generally it will have a plate on the back with holes corresponding to each string, so push the strings out through these and dispose of.

Now you're ready to attach the new strings:

1. On an acoustic, insert the ball-end of the E^{1st} string into the correct hole and wedge it in with a string peg. On an electric, thread it through the correct hole in the back-plate, coming up the E^{1st} aperture on the bridge.

2. Maintaining a bit of tension, stretch the string up toward the correct machine head and insert, leaving a little extra slack so that it will wind around the peg several times.

3. Slip the peg-winder over the tuning key and turn the handle vigorously to the right, while holding the string in place. The slack will be taken up, and the note will begin to rise as the string tightens. Get it close to the pitch it needs to be, but not all the way.

4. Repeat the process with the other five strings, from thinnest to thickest.

5. Be sure to turn each tuning key the same way. Use your tuner now, to bring each string up to pitch.

   Manually yank upward each string, all the way along the length of it, to work out the rest of the slack, otherwise the tuning will continue to slip.

   A final retune and you should be good to go!

One more chord to go: **F Major 7th** (F△).

F Major 7th

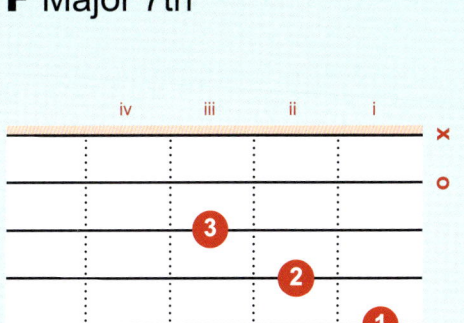
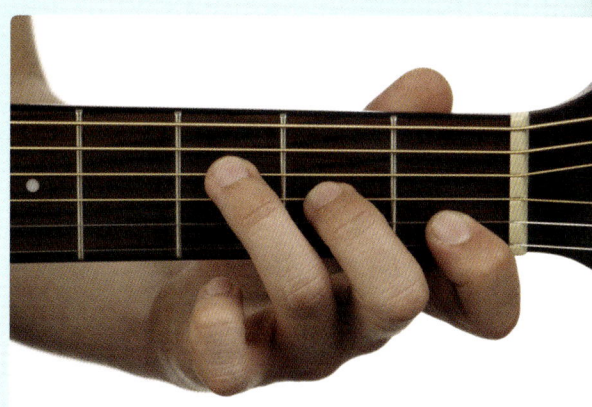

Go back to your chord of C. Keeping finger 1 where it is, now move fingers 2 and 3 down one string (toward the floor).

CHORD SEQUENCE: C - F△ - C - F△

Count yourself in: 1, 2, 3, 4, then strum the chord on the first beat of the next bar:

1	2	3	4		1	2	3	4		1	2	3	4		1	2	3	4
C				-	F△				-	C				-	F△			

LEVEL ONE

TUNING UP

There is no shame in using a guitar tuner—it's a vital bit of kit. However, when someone's "borrowed" your tuner (they do tend to walk!), you should also have the know-how to tune by ear.

- Play the sixth string—bottom E—from fret 5, followed by an open A string. Same note.
- Play the fifth string—A—from fret 5, followed by an open D string. Same note.
- Play the fourth string—D—from fret 5, followed by an open G string. Same note.
- There's always one exception, and it's the G string. Play it from the fourth fret to get the same note as the next open string, the B.
- Play the second string—B—from fret 5, followed by an open top E string. Same note again.
- So, as long as you have the correct note—an E, to tune bottom E to, you can tune the rest of the guitar from that one note, just making sure the pitch of each next open string corresponds with the pitch of the string before it, when played from the fifth fret (except the G, which is the fourth).

It's a good idea to acquaint yourself with the first five notes on each string from bottom to top. You'll make a better musician of yourself, and understand better how this quirky little tuning trick happens. Here they are:

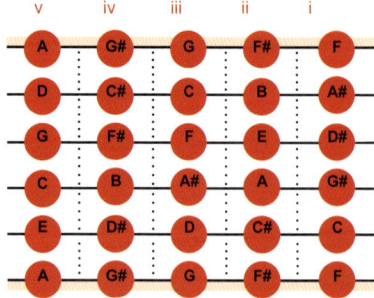

ROAD TEST

Here's one mighty sequence made up of all ten chords you've just learned.

The stickers are off—here comes the highway!

1	2	3	4	1	2	3	4	1	2	3	4	1	2	3	4
Am			-	Am			-	E			-	Em			

1	2	3	4	1	2	3	4	1	2	3	4	1	2	3	4
Am			-	Am7			-	E			-	E7			

1	2	3	4	1	2	3	4	1	2	3	4	1	2	3	4
Am			-	C			-	C△			-	G6			

1	2	3	4	1	2	3	4	1	2	3	4	1	2	3	4
F△			-	C			-	G6			-	G7			

1	2	3	4	1	2	3	4	1	2	3	4	1	2	3	4
C			-	F△			-	C			-	F△			

1	2	3	4	1	2	3	4	1	2	3	4	1	2	3	4
C			-	G7			-	C			-	C			

YAY—YOU'RE NOW A TROGG!

LEVEL TWO: QUO

Welcome to level two. Here, we will teach you how to count time in eighth beats and play your next ten chords. We'll also show you how to read a tab, and how to improvise.

It only took three chords—but Status Quo had those three chords "rockin' all over the world!"

Left: Status Quo guitarist Francis Rossi

LEVEL TWO

COUNTING TIME: **4/4 EIGHTH BEATS**

Count this aloud, at an even pace:

1AND**2**AND**3**AND**4**AND

Each of these beats is an eighth of a bar (in musical notation, one quaver).

Here are ten more chords, in five short sequences.

A Major

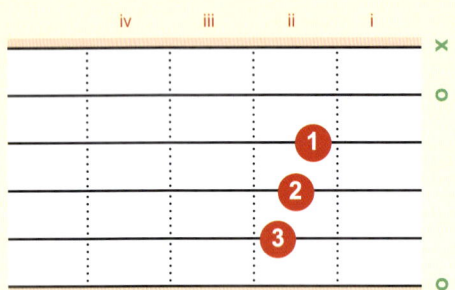

This is **A Major** (referred to as **A**).

For A, your fingers all fall within the same fret, so squash up!

A dominant 7th

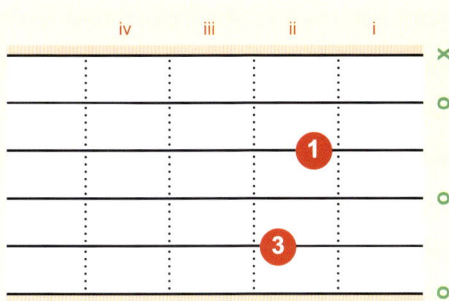

This is **A dominant 7th** (written as **A⁷**).

Once you have mastered A, simply remove your middle finger to turn the chord into A⁷.

STRUMMING: **THREE IN THE BAR**

Now, remembering your count of **1**AND**2**AND**3**AND**4**AND, practice this sequence three strums to the bar. These strums are all downstrokes (toward the floor)—for now. The strums fall on the numbers you count—the "ands" are in between strums.

CHORD SEQUENCE

You are going to count yourself in for one bar, then strum the A on the 1, 2, and 3 of the next bar, like this:

(count) **1**AND**2**AND**3**AND**4**AND

Strum AND **Strum** AND **Strum** AND **4** AND

Now, you're going to change chord to A⁷ on the fourth beat of the bar, and strum it on the first three beats of the next bar, before going back to A for the third bar. So count it in slowly and buy yourself some time. It's important you stay in rhythm. Like this:

1&	2&	3&	4&		1&	2&	3&	4&		1&	2&	3&	4&		1&	2&	3&	4&
Count				-	A	A	A		-	A⁷	A⁷	A⁷		-	A	A	A	

LEVEL TWO

D Major

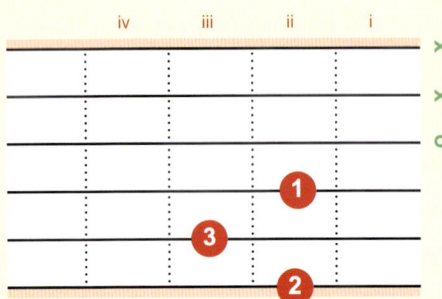
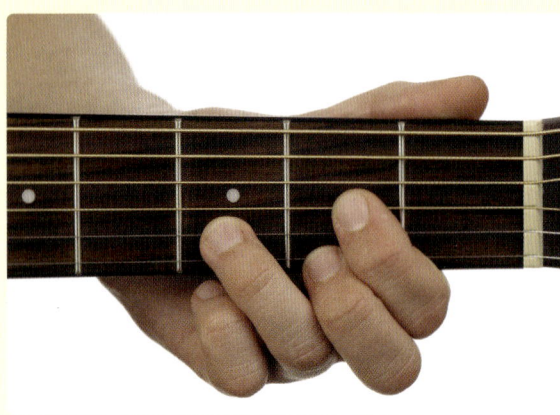

For **D Major** (written as **D**), form a mental image of the chord as a triangle. Got the D in place? Hold it there.

D minor

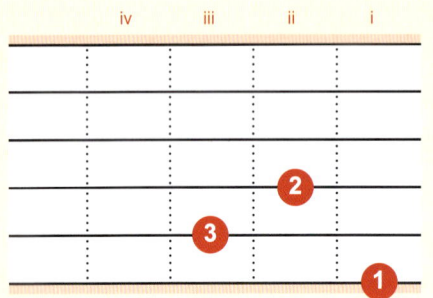
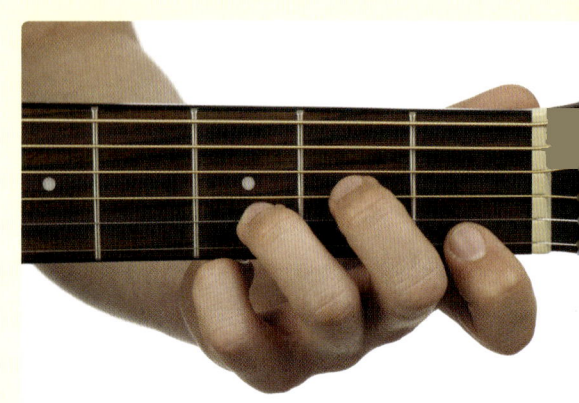

For **D minor** (referred to as **Dm**), don't move finger 3; leave it where it is on the third fret of the B string. Just move fingers 1 and 2.

Be sure to pay close attention to the small **x**s on the right-hand side of the fingerboard diagrams, which denote when a string is not to be strummed. These are **D** chords, so they are strummed from the **D** string. It's easy to fail to pay attention to your strumming hand, when all your focus is on the fingers of the chord hand. But don't strum all the strings from bottom E, or your D chord will not be D-lightful, it will be D-sgusting!

CHORD SEQUENCE: D - Dm - D

Count yourself in: 1, 2, 3, 4, then strum the chord on the first three beats of the next bar. Keep it really slow, so that you can make the chord change and stay in time rather than have an almighty pause:

1&	2&	3&	4&		1&	2&	3&	4&		1&	2&	3&	4&		1&	2&	3&	4&
Count				-	D	D	D		-	Dm	Dm	Dm		-	D	D	D	

D dominant 7th

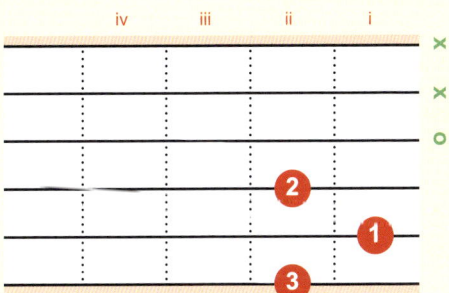

For **D dominant 7th** (referred to as **D⁷**), form a mental image of the chord as an **inverted** (or upside down) triangle.

LEVEL TWO

A Major 7th

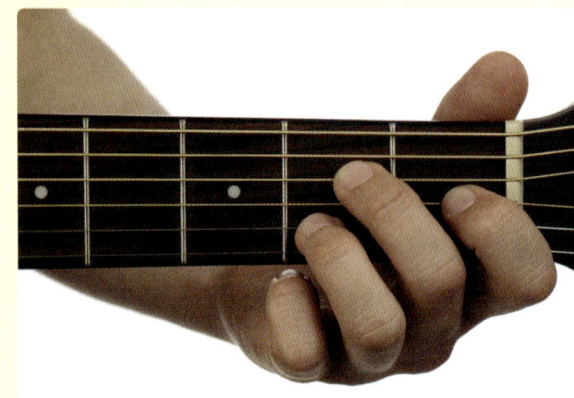

Got the D⁷ in place? Hold it there. For **A Major 7th** (written as **A**ᐃ), simply move the whole shape up (toward the ceiling) by one string. It becomes Aᐃ.

B dominant 7th

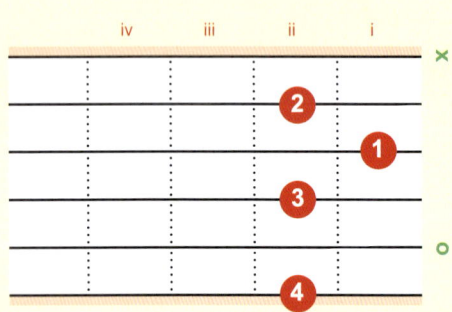

Got the A⁷ in place? For **B dominant 7th** (referred to as **B⁷**), again just move the whole shape up (toward the ceiling) by one string. Now, put finger 4 on the second fret of top E.

CHORD SEQUENCE: D7 - A△ - B7

Count yourself in: 1, 2, 3, 4, then strum the chord on the first three beats of the next bar.

This sequence is essentially just one shape moving upward by a string, to become the next chord.

1&	2&	3&	4&	1&	2&	3&	4&	1&	2&	3&	4&	1&	2&	3&	4&
Count				-	D⁷	D⁷	D⁷	-	A△	A△	A△	-	B⁷	B⁷	B⁷

B minor

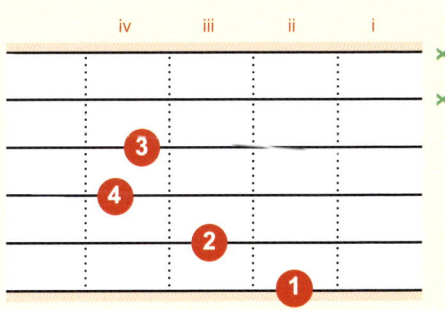

For **B minor** (written as **Bᵐ**), get finger 1 in place first, then make an Aᵐ shape on the strings above it, with your remaining fingers.

LEVEL TWO

C minor

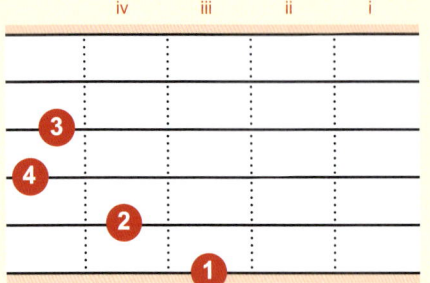

For **C minor** (referred to as **C^m**), simply move the whole B^m shape one fret further up the fretboard. Don't lift your fingers off to change chord, just release the pressure and slide up a semitone/fret.

CHORD SEQUENCE: B^m - C^m - B^m

Count yourself in: **1AND2AND3AND4AND** then strum the chord on the first three beats of the next bar.

1&	2&	3&	4&		1&	2&	3&	4&		1&	2&	3&	4&		1&	2&	3&	4&
Count				-	B^m	B^m	B^m		-	C^m	C^m	C^m		-	B^m	B^m	B^m	

HOW TO READ A **TAB**

In this book, Guitar Tab will be used to write single-note sequences. It's a form widely used by guitarists, as it is so much easier to read and learn than formal, "old school" musical notation. We will gradually introduce tab symbols to guide your technique, but for now, here is a Guitar Tab in its most basic form.

Tab is short for tablature, and is written on the left-hand side. As with the fingerboard diagrams, the horizontal lines represent your strings, but this time, the lowest E is at the bottom and top E at the top! It's easy to remember it's that way around because the word "tab" has B at the bottom and T at the top!

Fret numbers are placed on the guitar string lines, to show you where to put your fingers, in sequence, reading from left to right.

So let's start with a scale. The stickers will be handy for you to mark out on your guitar where to play your notes. But remember, there will be open strings as well.

SCALE OF **C MAJOR**

- A scale is made up of eight notes. This tab tells us the first note of the C Major scale is the third fret of the A string.
- The second note is an O, which tells us to play the D string "open"—i.e., no finger at all. The third and fourth notes of the scale are on the same string, second fret, then third.
- Fifth note is open G, sixth note is G, second fret. Seventh note is open B, eighth is B first fret.
- Try it this way: put your fingers on the fretboard in the shape of a **C chord**. Now your fingers are lined up in the correct position to play this scale. Use finger 3 to play the fret 3 notes, finger 2 to play the frot 2 notes, and finger 1 to play the fret 1 notes.
- When it is an open string note, simply lift up that finger from the string.

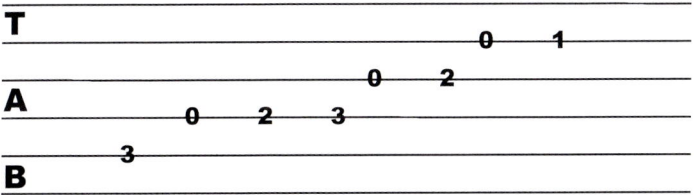

LEVEL TWO

HOW TO **IMPROVISE**

THE THREE-CHORD TRICK

"It goes like this, the fourth, the fifth / The minor fall, the Major lift."

So sings Leonard Cohen in his brilliant and much-loved classic "Hallelujah."

Cleverly, he's actually singing about the chord progression at that very moment of his song. And it tells us everything we need to know about modern music because, from rock 'n' roll through fifty years of pop and rock to the present day, almost every song is more or less structured around three chords. Starting with the blues, the three-chord trick developed and cross-pollinated into every contemporary musical form.

Whatever key you're in, you just need to know the eight notes of the scale for that key, then make a Major chord out of the first, the fourth, and the fifth. It's that easy, and that's why you need to learn your scales!

Once you know what key you're in and figure out these three chords, it's possible to improvise your way through almost any song you hear.

So, we are going to make a Major chord out of three notes of the scale of C Major: the first, the fourth, and the fifth. The first note of the scale is the root (or tonic)—the note after which the scale is named. So the "first" in this case is a C.

If you follow the scale of notes up through the key—first (C), second (D), third (E), you arrive at F—the fourth note in the scale. Then G, the fifth.

So the three Major chords we need are C, F, and G.

We will learn more scales and figure out their three relevant Major chords (and relative minors) later in this book. But if you master this early lesson in the musical process, it will soon be possible, by ear, to anticipate where almost every single track you attempt to learn is going to go, because believe it or not, all the songs you know, love, and wish you could play are fundamentally structured around the first, the fourth, and the fifth.

It's the old three-chord trick!

G Major

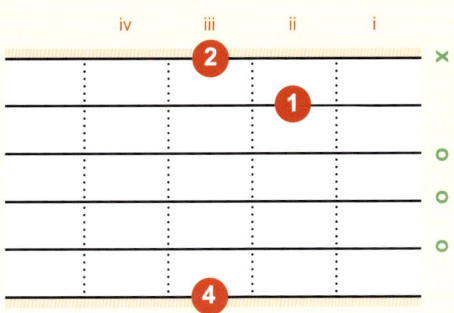

For **G Major** (written as **G**), place finger 1 on the A string on fret 2, finger 2 on the E^{6th} string on fret 3, and finger 4 on the E^{1st} string, also on fret 3.

ROAD TEST

You now have twenty chords. So let's string a few together.

Here are some chord sequences.

On this first one, three strums per bar, apart from the fourth bar, where you strum the first beat of the bar only.

CHORD SEQUENCE: A - D - E

1&	2&	3&	4&	1&	2&	3&	4&	1&	2&	3&	4&	1&	2&	3&	4&
A	A	A	-	D	D	D	-	E	E	E	-	A			

Let's now try strumming these chords a bit differently.

Think slow, slow—quick-quick—slow, slow—quick-quick.

Think: "Wild Thing!"

SLOW	SLOW	QUICK	QUICK	SLOW	SLOW	QUICK	QUICK
A	A	D	D	E	E	D	D

LEVEL TWO

Now use the same chords as the last exercise, but slightly rearranged. Repeating them round and round, you can play these chords alongside "Chasing Cars" by Snow Patrol.

Strum one in the bar:

CHORD SEQUENCE: A - E - D

1&	2&	3&	4&		1&	2&	3&	4&		1&	2&	3&	4&		1&	2&	3&	4&
A				-	A				-	E				-	E			

1&	2&	3&	4&		1&	2&	3&	4&		1&	2&	3&	4&		1&	2&	3&	4&
D				-	D				-	A				-	A			

Frontman Gary Lightbody wrote "Chasing Cars" in the garden after drinking a bottle of wine. He has since said that it's "the most pure and open love song I've ever written." It was voted record of the decade in the UK in 2009.

Try playing this sequence along to "Creep" by Radiohead.

One strum on the first beat of each bar:

CHORD SEQUENCE: G - B⁷ - C - Cᵐ

1&	2&	3&	4&		1&	2&	3&	4&		1&	2&	3&	4&		1&	2&	3&	4&
G				-	G				-	B⁷				-	B⁷			

1&	2&	3&	4&		1&	2&	3&	4&		1&	2&	3&	4&		1&	2&	3&	4&
C				-	C				-	Cᵐ				-	Cᵐ			

Song composer Thom Yorke (Radiohead's lead singer) wrote "Creep" in 1987 when a student at Exeter University (UK). He says it's about being in love with someone, but not feeling good enough. "There's beautiful people," he says, "and then there's the rest of us."

LEVEL TWO

It's not easy to sound like Jimi Hendrix, but this will get you started. Play this sequence on repeat as you listen to "Hey Joe."

The bars are quite a bit faster on this one, so count 1, 2, 3, 4. And there are five chords involved this time. The last chord is strummed for four consecutive bars: one strum on the first beat of each bar.

CHORD SEQUENCE: C - G - D - A - E

1&	2&	3&	4&	1&	2&	3&	4&	1&	2&	3&	4&	1&	2&	3&	4&
C			-	G			-	D			-	A			

1&	2&	3&	4&	1&	2&	3&	4&	1&	2&	3&	4&	1&	2&	3&	4&
E			-	E			-	E			-	E			

WOAH! YOU'RE A QUO!

"Hey Joe" was Hendrix's first single. An unimpressed Dick Rowe of Decca Records turned down Hendrix for a record deal when he heard it (four years earlier, he turned down The Beatles!). It has been recorded by more than 400 artists.

RIFF REWARD (QUO)

Congratulations, you've earned a Riff Reward!

The Deep Purple song "Smoke on the Water" tells the story of a Frank Zappa concert in Montreux, Switzerland, at which a member of the audience fired a couple of flares at the ceiling and burnt the place down. Deep Purple watched the drama unfold from a restaurant across the lake, which became shrouded in smoke—hence the title. Guitarist Ritchie Blackmore—a fan of Renaissance music—provided the riff. "It's done in fourths and fifths, a medieval modal scale, which makes it dark and foreboding," he said, "not like today's pop music thirds."

Four decades later, at Rok Skool Sussex where I teach, there isn't a wannabe guitarist that walks through the door who doesn't arrive dying to smash out the riff—usually while I'm talking!

Try this to get the same effect:

Two note chords played with fingers 2 and 3, plucked out by thumb and forefinger on two strings (D and G):

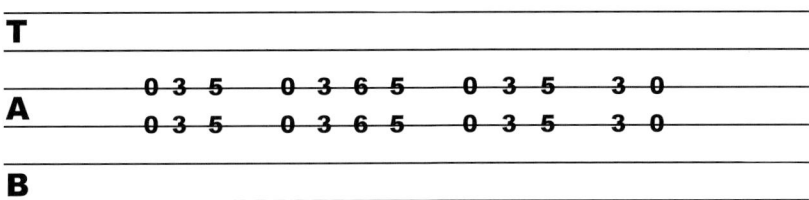

LEVEL THREE: FOO

In this level, we introduce another strumming technique and show you how to arpeggiate your chords. We'll also show you twenty more chords, plus power and barre chords. Additionally, you'll learn scales, and how to use them to predict the correct chords to play in any given key.

Gut-punching rock by Foo Fighters shows what can be achieved with just a bunch of chords and utter commitment.

Left: Dave Grohl of Foo Fighters

LEVEL THREE

COUNTING TIME: 6/8

So far, our bars have been in 4/4 time—four beats to the bar. Now we're going to look at 6/8 time—six beats to the bar.

Counting aloud, and with extra emphasis on the 4, try this:

1 2 3 **4** 5 6 — 1 2 3 **4** 5 6

STRUMMING: FOUR IN THE BAR 6/8 TIME

Using D, G, E^m, and A^7

Now strum the same rhythm, all downstrokes still, four strokes in a row, with the fourth one being a little louder than the other three. Use the chord of **D** (remembering to strum it from the D string) for two bars, then change to **G** for two bars.

CHORD SEQUENCE: D - G

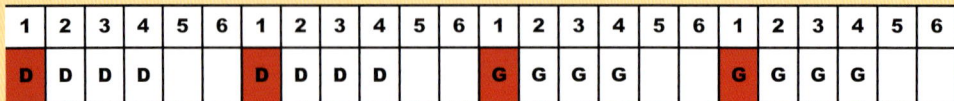

Now from **E^m** to **A^7**.

CHORD SEQUENCE: E^m - A^7

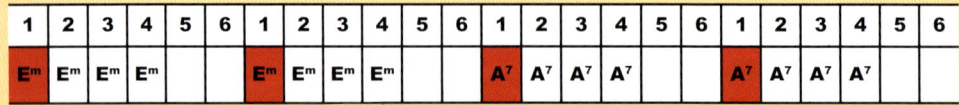

You can strum these chords along to R.E.M.'s "Everybody Hurts."

ARPEGGIATING A CHORD

Now let's use that same sequence to arpeggiate a chord. This is when we pluck the individual notes of the chord, in a sequence. If you've been using a plectrum until now, this is the time to set it aside. You are going to be plucking the strings with the thumb and forefinger (finger 1) of your strumming hand.

So, we had four strums of a D chord in bars one and two, which now become a (gentle):

- Downward thumb-pluck on the D string on beat 1
- Downward thumb-pluck on the G string on beat 2
- Upward finger 1-pluck on the B string on beat 3
- Upward finger 1-pluck on the top E string on beat 4
- And repeat, followed by two bars, with the G chord

So, you are moving in a downward direction (toward the floor) between finger and thumb, from the D string to the E string. Let's switch to our tab model (remember: B stands for bottom E, and the T for top E):

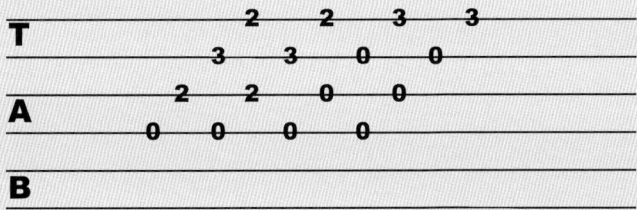

Now repeat the process with the **E**m to **A**7. This time, you're going to pluck from the root note of each of those chords—the Em from the E string, the A7 from the A string:

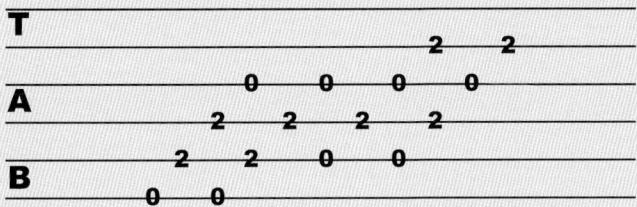

LEVEL THREE

MORE ARPEGGIATING IN 6/8

Arpeggiate down four strings from the root note of each chord on the first four beats of the bar, then change to the next chord on the two beats of that bar left to you. You are changing every bar this time, so think on your feet. Always stay in time, so keep it nice and slow until you can manage the chord changes more quickly. Each of these tab sequences is eight bars.

SEQUENCE: Using G, E^m

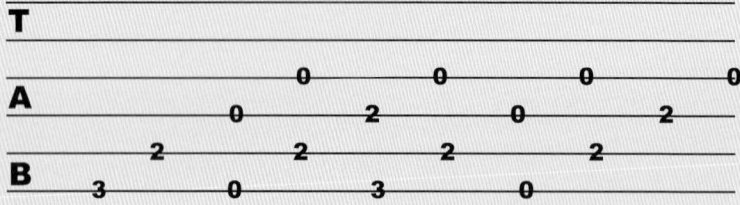

SEQUENCE: Using C, D, G, D

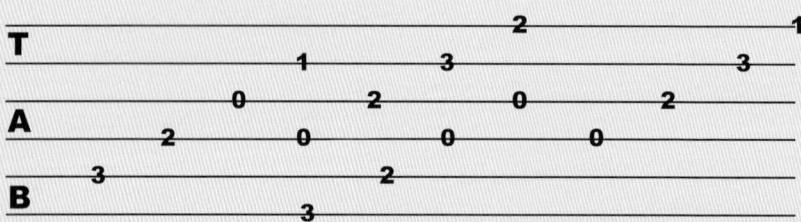

UPSTROKES, SYNCOPATED STRUMMING

It's time to upgrade your strumming technique. So far in this book, everything has been on a downstroke (toward the floor). This time, you are going to strum using upstrokes (toward the ceiling), too, on eighth-beats, to give a more syncopated, groovy rhythm.

UP AND DOWN, SYNCOPATED STRUMMING

CHORD SEQUENCE: C - F△ - Aᵐ

Count this out loud, putting extra emphasis on the 1, and the AND after the 2:

1AND2**AND**3AND4AND—**1**AND2**AND**3AND4AND

Now do it strumming a chord on those two eighth beats of the bar. Use a **downstroke** on the **1** (↓) and an **upstroke** on the **AND** (↑).

1	AND	2	AND	3	AND	4	AND	1	AND	2	AND	3	AND	4	AND
↓C			↑C					↓C			↑C				

1	AND	2	AND	3	AND	4	AND	1	AND	2	AND	3	AND	4	AND
↓F△			↑F△					↓F△			↑F△				

Play the above sequence twice, then this next sequence twice, and repeat.

1	AND	2	AND	3	AND	4	AND	1	AND	2	AND	3	AND	4	AND
↓Aᵐ			↑Aᵐ					↓C			↑C				

1	AND	2	AND	3	AND	4	AND	1	AND	2	AND	3	AND	4	AND
↓F△			↑F△					↓F△			↑F△				

Sounds like . . . "Use Somebody," by Kings of Leon.

LEVEL THREE

CHORD SEQUENCE: $F^\triangle$ - G^7 - C - A^{m7}

Count this aloud, emphasizing the bold-faced eighth beats:

1AND**2**AND**3**AND**4****AND**

Strum: this is slightly more challenging! Your first strum is downstroke (↓) falling on the 1 of the bar. Your next strum—an upstroke, falls on the AND after the 4, at the end of the bar—in other words, just ahead of the second bar. In muso terms, this second chord is "pushed."

Try a bar like this—count slowly (and continue to count the next bar, even though it has no chord in it):

1	AND	2	AND	3	AND	4	AND		1	AND	2	AND	3	AND	4	AND
↓$F^\triangle$							↑G^7	-						-		

Now do chords three and four of this sequence, in the same way.

1	AND	2	AND	3	AND	4	AND		1	AND	2	AND	3	AND	4	AND
↓$C^\triangle$							↑A^{m7}	-								

Now play this sequence with a busier strum—downstrokes on the 1, 2, 3 of the bar, swiftly followed by the upstroke.

1	AND	2	AND	3	AND	4	AND		1	AND	2	AND	3	AND	4	AND
↓$F^\triangle$		↓$F^\triangle$		↓$F^\triangle$			↑G^7	-								

1	AND	2	AND	3	AND	4	AND		1	AND	2	AND	3	AND	4	AND
↓$C^\triangle$		↓$C^\triangle$		↓$C^\triangle$			↑A^{m7}	-								

This chord sequence is a perfect accompaniment to Coldplay's "Viva La Vida" . . .

"Viva la Vida" literally means "The Life Lives," and is the name of a painting by Frida Kahlo that inspired Chris Martin's lyric about being judged on your life, at the end of it all. The lyrics are anti-authoritarian in nature, and the challenging chord sequences could be said to represent the struggles of daily human life.

LEVEL THREE

POWERCHORDS

Most chords are essentially three notes of the scale, played together to make a pleasing sound—the first note (or root), the third note of the scale, and the fifth. Don't let this confuse you. To find the right three chords for a particular key, we look to the first, fourth, and fifth notes of a scale, a different thing entirely! But, as I say, most chords are a combination of three notes: the first, third, and fifth.

Powerchords, however, comprise only the root and the fifth, with a repetition of the root an octave up. It is the third that makes a chord so melodious. A chord without the third is not a pretty thing. It's kinda mean! It's also a much easier version of the barre chord—two reasons that make a powerchord the staple diet of every rock band in the world.

Pay close attention to the Roman numerals on all diagrams from here out. You are going to be shaping chords up and down the length of the fretboard.

POWERCHORD 1: **F**

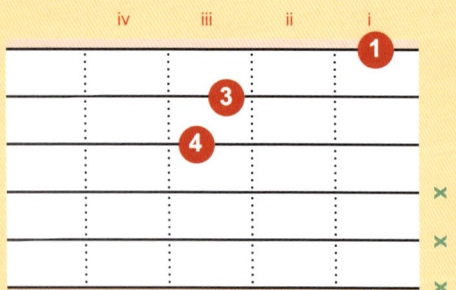

POWERCHORD 2: **A#**

Powerchord 2 is exactly the same as powerchord 1, but "in" a string.

The crucial thing is to only strum the three strings on which your fingers are pressing.

Both of these powerchord shapes can move up and down the fretboard. Finger 1 determines which Major chord it is. This is because it is on the root. So, in this case, powerchord 1 is an F, powerchord 2 is an A#.

Now do powerchord 1 followed by powerchord 2, three frets up: **G#** and **C#**.

POWERCHORD 1: **G#**

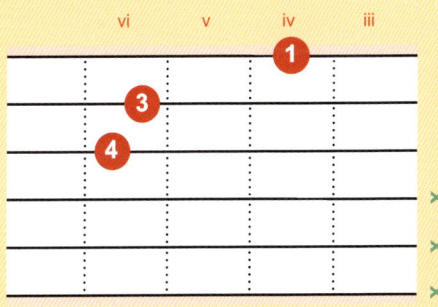

With powerchord 1 starting on the fourth fret, finger 1 is on G#, so our chord is G#.

LEVEL THREE

POWERCHORD 2: C#

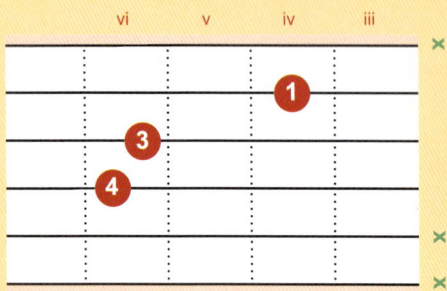

For powerchord 2, finger 1 is on C#, so our chord is C#.

You begin to see what a fantastically adaptable and versatile chord this is!

Now try this, a sequence of the last four chords (all downstrokes):

CHORD SEQUENCE:

1	AND	2	AND	3	AND	4	AND		1	AND	2	AND	3	AND	4	AND
F		F				A#	A#	-	G#		G#				C#	C#

Try this sequence alongside Nirvana's game-changing "Smells Like Teen Spirit"!

Nirvana's anthem for the grunge era "Smells Like Teen Spirit" was penned by the band's guru, Kurt Cobain. A girlfriend had graffitied "Kurt smells like teen spirit" on his bedroom wall and he turned the phrase into a song, little knowing "Teen Spirit" was the name of the scent she was wearing. Sales of the perfume rocketed!

LEVEL THREE

POWERCHORD 1: A

POWERCHORD 1: G

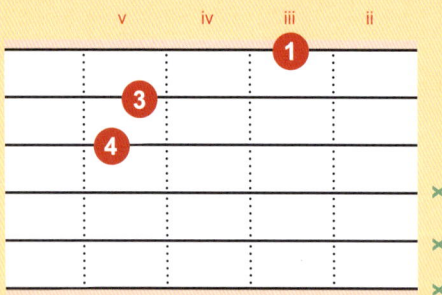

POWERCHORD 2: D

This one is against a slow count, played in sequence, round and round:

1	AND	2	AND	3	AND	4	AND	1	AND	2	AND	3	AND	4	AND
A	A			G	G			-	D	D		D	D		

Alanis Morrisette's raging *Jagged Little Pill* album contains songs to belt out your power chords to. Crank "You Oughta Know" or "Forgiven" up loud and wait for the chorus to come storming in—and the neighbors to come storming down the garden path!

LEVEL THREE

Red Hot Chili Peppers' "Dani California" won a Grammy in 2007 for best pop song. The guitar riff is more than similar to one in a Tom Petty song, but Petty didn't sue. "A lot of rock 'n' roll songs sound the same," he said magnanimously.

POWERCHORD 2: C

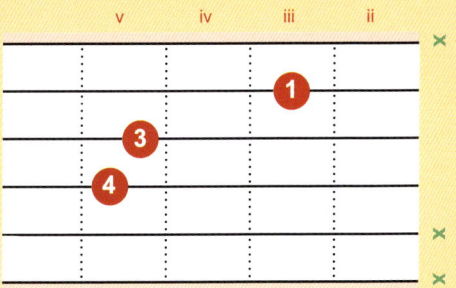

Here's another sequence, but try a different rhythm. Think slow, slow—quick-quick—slow, slow—quick-quick:

1	AND	2	AND	3	AND	4	AND	1	AND	2	AND	3	AND	4	AND
F		F				C	C		-	D		D			G	G	

Congratulations! You've now harnessed the playing style of the Red Hot Chili Peppers!

LEVEL THREE

BARRE CHORDS

Finger 1, be strong, your time has come! Barre chords are so-called because your first finger will form a bar (just as a capo does) across all the strings. It takes strength to apply the necessary pressure so that all the strings ring out.

Once in place, fingers 2, 3, and 4 will then form a selection of chords in front of finger 1—E Majors, E minors, A minors, C Majors, A Majors— all shapes you know well. These can then be moved up and down the fretboard.

In effect, finger 1 is imitating the nut and allowing you to play your chords in multiple positions up and down the neck.

Suddenly, you have many, many more chords at your disposal, along the whole length of the fretboard.

The barre chord becomes easier to play the further up the neck we play it, as the frets are closer together and less pressure is needed on the strings. So to start, we are going to site these next shapes at fret 5.

BARRE CHORD: **A**

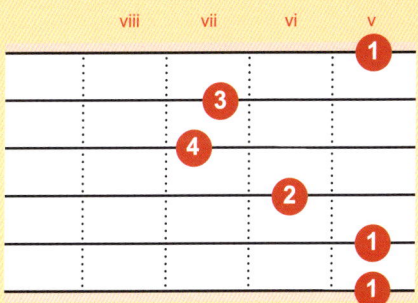

So, finger 1 across the fifth fret. With your remaining fingers, form an E shape in front of it. In this position, the barre chord you are playing is an **A Major**.

BARRE CHORD: **Aᵐ**

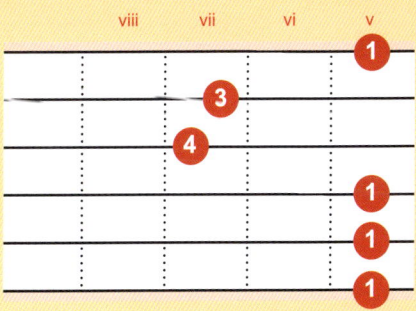

Now take off finger 2. You'll see your fingers have made an E minor in front of finger 1. In this position, the barre chord you are playing is an **A minor**.

LEVEL THREE

BARRE CHORD: D^m

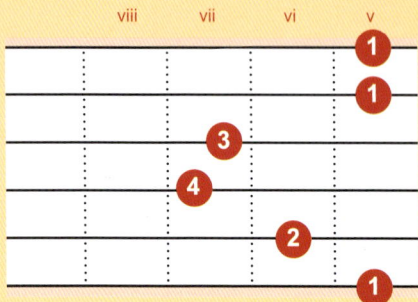
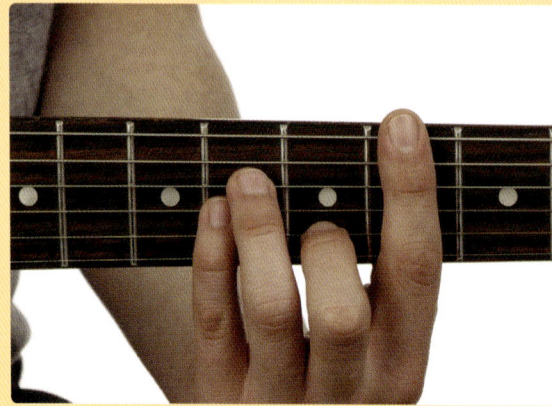

Now form an A minor shape in front of finger 1. In this position, the barre chord you are playing is **D minor**.

BARRE CHORD: D

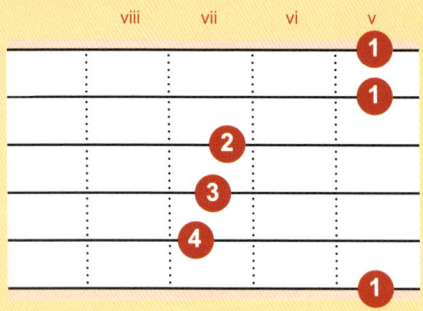

Keep finger 1 across the fifth fret. With your remaining fingers, form an A Major in front of it. In this position, the barre chord you are playing is **D Major**.

You may be wondering why an A Major shape is suddenly a D? That's because you are playing that A chord **five semitones higher**, which makes it a D.

BARRE CHORD: B

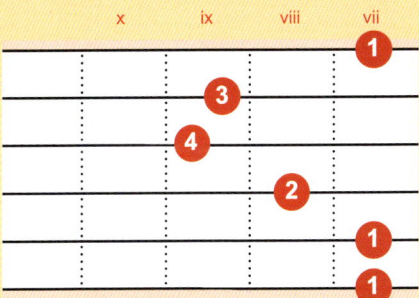

Now let's go back to your first barre chord, finger 1 with the E Major shape in front of it. But this time, build it up on the seventh fret. This is the chord of **B Major**.

BARRE CHORD: F

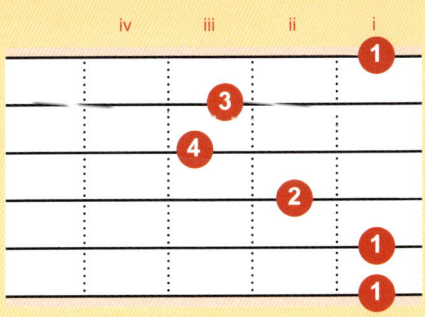

Now move the whole shape down to fret 1. The barre chord you are now playing is an **F Major**.

LEVEL THREE

BARRE: F^m

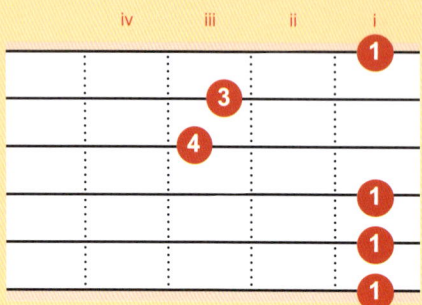

Staying on the first fret, take off finger 2. You now have an E minor shape in front of finger 1, and the barre chord you are playing is an **F minor**.

BARRE: G

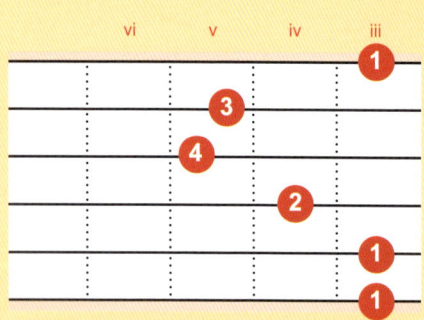

Now move up two frets to the third fret. Build an E shape in front of finger 1. The barre chord you are now playing is **G Major**.

After you've played this chord, go back to the "open" form of G that you already learned. You can hear they're the same. **You can have more than one way to play a chord on the guitar.** All of the open chords you have learned can be reproduced in other locations further up the neck as barre chords.

Meanwhile, two of the earlier chords you learned in this book—B minor and C minor—were "cut-down." So, here are the full barre chord versions.

BARRE:
B^m on second fret

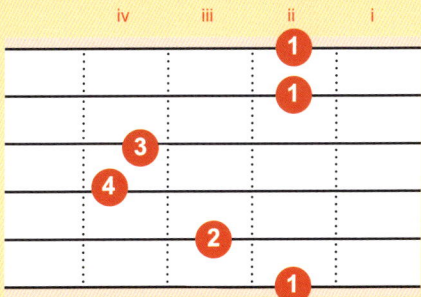

B minor builds on the second fret with an A minor shape in front of finger 1.

BARRE:
C^m on third fret

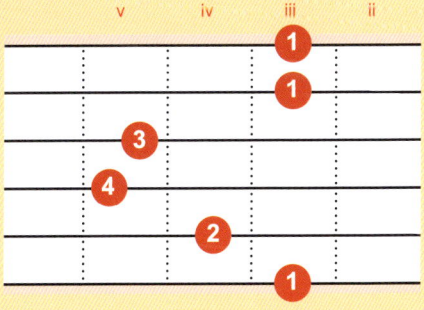
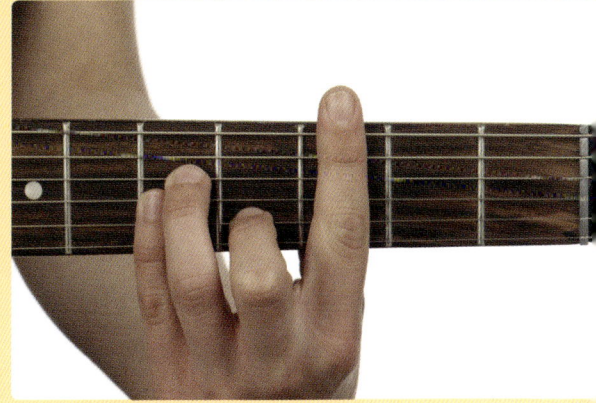

C minor builds on the third fret with an A minor shape in front of finger 1.

LEVEL THREE

And different versions of both these chords can be played as barre chords higher up the neck . . .

BARRE:
B^m on seventh fret

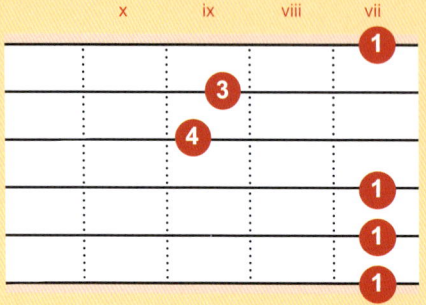

B minor builds on the seventh fret with an E minor shape in front of finger 1.

BARRE:
C^m on eighth fret

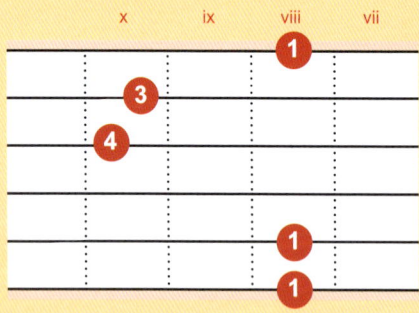

C minor builds on the eighth fret with a G minor shape in front of finger 1.

If you carry on up the fretboard with this shape, you get C#m, then Dm, then D#m . . . see how versatile these barre chords are?

FOUR MORE SCALES:

Three Major and Three Relative Minor Chords

Previously, we discussed the three-chord trick and how a Major chord formed on first, fourth, and fifth notes of any given scale gives you the three "right" Major chords for playing in that key. We applied it to the scale of C Major—the only scale we have looked at, up to this point.

Now we are going to examine four more keys and their Major scales, and identify their three "right" Majors.

Every Major chord has a relative minor. So we are also going to learn how to find the three "right" minor chords associated with that key.

For the first time in this book, we are traveling in a downward direction, so look out for flat signs instead of sharps. Refer back to page 11 for more on sharps and flats.

SCALE: G Major

1st G – 2nd A – 3rd B – 4th C – 5th D – 6th E – 7th F# – 8th G

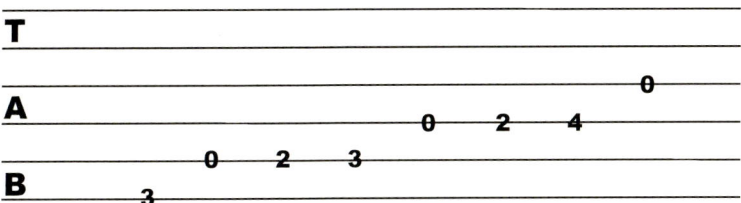

The **1st** is **G**, **4th C**, and **5th D**.

Our three Majors for the **key of G** are therefore **G–C–D**.

How to find the **relative minor**: go down three semitones from the root note of the Major chord and make a minor chord—it's that simple.

So, to find the relative minor for G Major, go down three semitones: one semitone down is G♭, then F, then E. You have arrived, so make a minor chord on E. You now know that the **relative minor** for **G Major** is **E minor**.

Do the same for C Major. One semitone down is B, then B♭, then A. You have arrived, so make a minor chord on A. The **relative minor** for **C Major** is **A minor**.

Do the same for D Major. One semitone down is D♭, then C, then B. Make a minor chord on B. The **relative minor** for **D Major** is **B minor**.

SCALE: D Major

1st D – 2nd E – 3rd F# – 4th G – 5th A – 6th B – 7th C# – 8th D

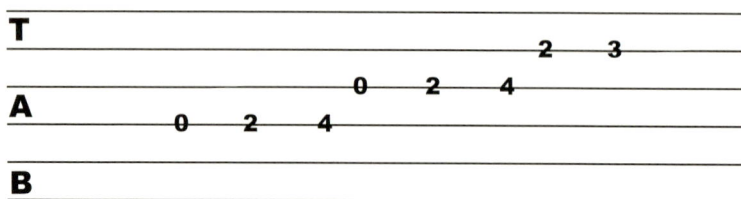

The **1st** is **D**, **4th G**, and **5th A**, so three "right" Major chords for **key of D** are: **D–G–A**.

Relative minor:

D Major: B minor.

G Major: E minor.

A Major: go down three semitones: A♭, then G, then G♭. The relative minor is G♭ minor. (G♭ is the same as F#.)

SCALE: A Major

1st A – 2nd B – 3rd C# – 4th D – 5th E – 6th F# – 7th G# – 8th A

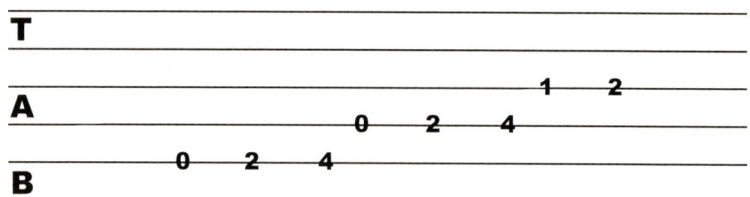

The **1st** is **A**, **4th D**, and **5th E**, so three "right" Major Chords for **key of A** are: **A–D–E**.

Relative minor:

A Major: G♭ minor.

D Major: B minor.

E Major: go down three semitones: E♭, then D, then D♭. The relative minor is **D♭ minor**. (D♭ is the same as C#.)

SCALE: E Major

1st E – 2nd F# – 3rd G# – 4th A – 5th B – 6th C# – 7th D# – 8th E

```
T|---------------------------------|
A|-----------------------1---2-----|
B|-----------0---2---4-------------|
 |---0---2---4---------------------|
```

The **1st** is **E**, **4th A**, and **5th B**, so three "right" Major chords for **key of E** are: **E–A–B**.

Relative minor:

E Major: D♭ minor.

A Major: G♭ minor.

B Major: go down three semitones: B♭, then A, then A♭. The relative minor is **A♭ minor**. (A♭ is the same as G#.)

Now you have three Major and three minor chords that sound great in their particular key. That's six chords—more than enough to write a great song, and more than enough to busk your way through virtually any song you hear in any of the five keys you've covered.

WOO-HOO—YOU'RE A FOO!

LEVEL THREE

RIFF REWARD (FOO)

Congratulations, you've earned a Riff Reward!

The number that inspires this riff is a creation of Jack White. "Seven Nation Army" is what he thought the Salvation Army was called when he was a kid.

The White Stripes had no bass player. The riff is actually just guitar, but a guitar going through an octave pedal to send it an octave down. Try playing along with these chords. The numbers below the tab refer to which finger you need to use.

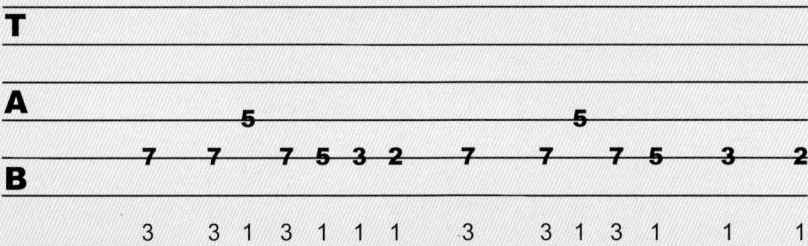

When the chorus comes in, you can bang out the same riff with powerchord 2s (when a chord is shown in tab, the notes are stacked one on top of the other):

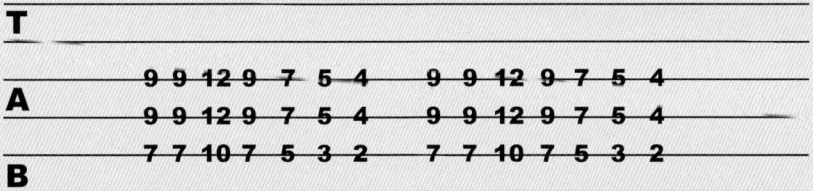

Left: Jack White of The White Stripes

LEVEL FOUR: ZEP

Here, you will find seventy-five more chords, arranged according to their family groups: dominant 7ths, Major 7ths, minor 7ths, and sus 4ths. We will also introduce you to the CAGED chord system and the pentatonic scale.

Guitar wizardry underpins Led Zeppelin's brand of rock. This is musicianship to aspire to.

Left: Led Zeppelin guitarist Jimmy Page

LEVEL FOUR

CHORD **FAMILIES**

Before the barre chords, all twenty chords you'd learned were arranged in the easiest way to get you from one to the other. Now it's time to meet the family!

Just as members of the same family all have a shared look, members of a chord family all have a shared sound—the sleepy summer's day of the Major 7ths, the sadness of minors and positivity of Majors; the pop sensibilities of dominant 7ths and sus 4ths, and the jazziness of the 9ths—a family you have yet to meet!

Some of these chords you have already met, but there are many new ones here. Use the stickers if you need them to help you remember these new chords.

The same chord can be found and played in multiple positions, so we offer them here both open and barred. And as you shall see, there are two different versions of a barre chord in many instances, depending on whether the root is on the E string or the A string.

DOMINANT **7THS**

These chords are rarely referred to as dominant 7ths by guitarists—they call them just 7ths. And the seventh element can either be placed high in the chord, or an octave lower in the chord, so while they share the familial "sound," they both have a different color. Like this:

E^{7th} (high)

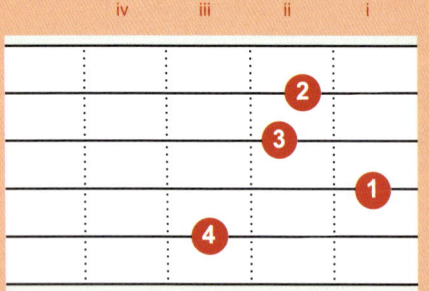

Here, you are playing a normal E Major, but turning it into a 7th by adding the seventh note at the top end of the chord's register.

78

E⁷ᵗʰ (low)

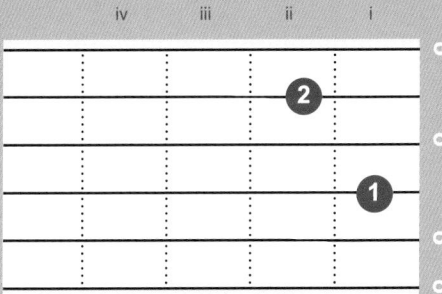

Here, you are playing a normal E Major, but turning it into a 7th by leaving off finger 3. The open D now gives you the seventh, but an octave lower in the chord's register. Hear the similarity? Hear the difference?

E⁷ᵗʰ (barre)

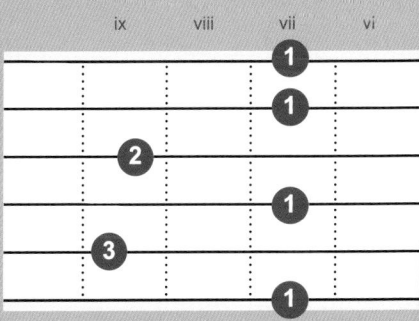

Here's the trickier barre chord version, higher up the neck.

LEVEL FOUR

Playing these chords in different positions depends on:

a) Where the chords around it are falling. You don't want to be covering unnecessary distance from one chord to another—something that will compromise your timing.

b) The color, the flavor that each differently shaped version of the chord imparts to your song. How do you want it to sound in that moment?

c) If you're playing in a band with a second guitarist, which version of the chord is he/she playing? Because you need to be playing a different one!

Now, let's do the same thing with A^{7th}.

A^{7th} (high)

Here, you are playing a normal A Major, but turning it into a 7th by adding the seventh note at the top end of the chord's register.

A⁷ᵗʰ (low)

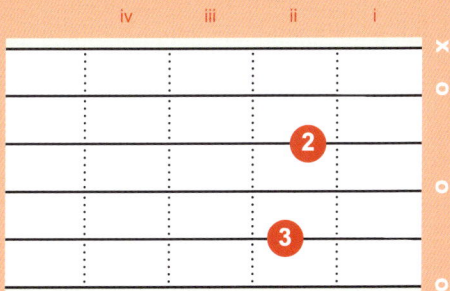
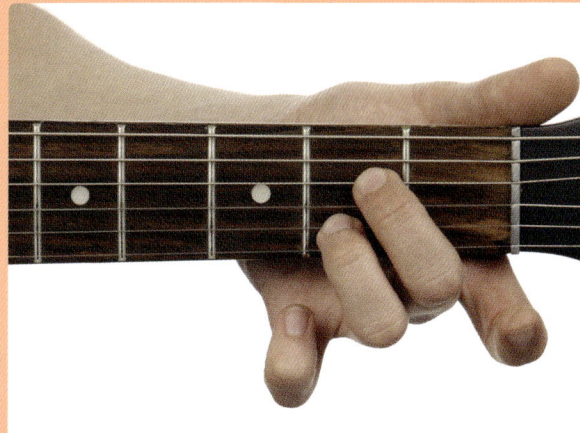

Here, you are playing a normal A Major, but with a gap in the middle!
And the open G now provides you with the seventh.

A⁷ᵗʰ (barre)

Here's the trickier barre chord version, higher up the neck.

LEVEL FOUR

D⁷ᵗʰ (open)

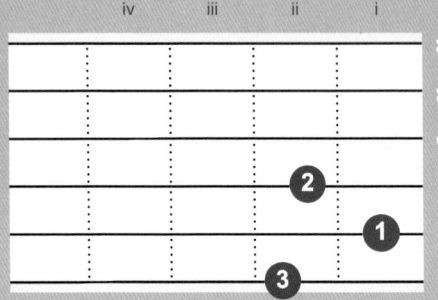

D⁷ᵗʰ
(barre, root on A string)

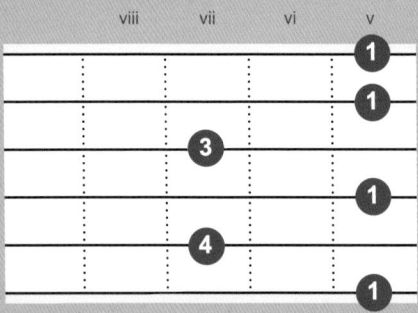

D⁷ᵗʰ
(barre, root on E string, low 7th)

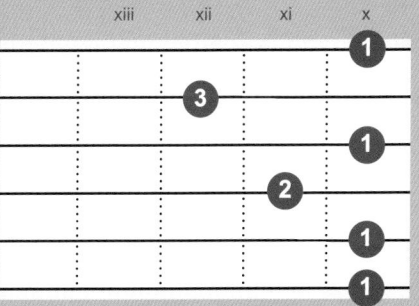

D⁷ᵗʰ
(barre, root on E string, high 7th)

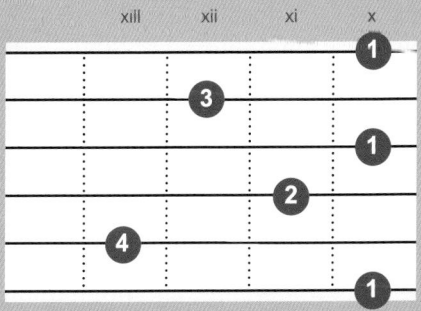

LEVEL FOUR

Four positions for G⁷ᵗʰ now:

G⁷ᵗʰ
(open)

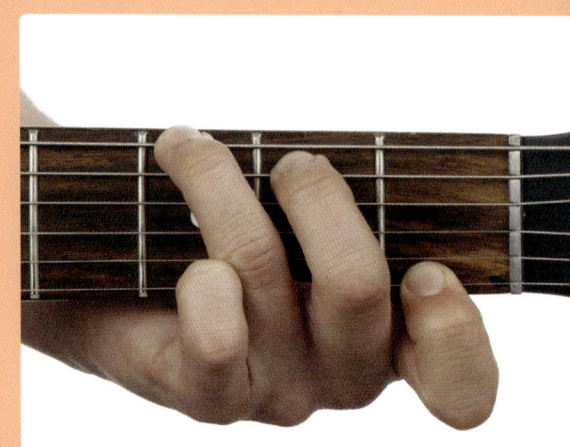

G⁷ᵗʰ
(barre, root on E string, low 7th)

Barre using an E shape with one finger left off, to give you a low 7th on an open string.

G⁷ᵗʰ

(barre, root on E string, high 7th)

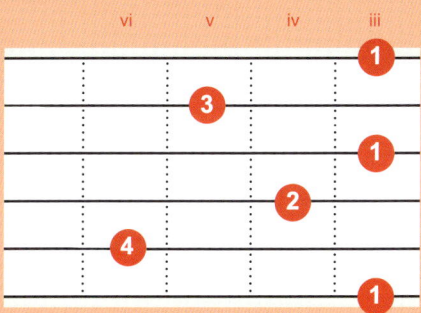

Barre using an E shape with finger 4 added to the top of the chord, to give you a high 7th.

G⁷ᵗʰ

(barre, root on A string)

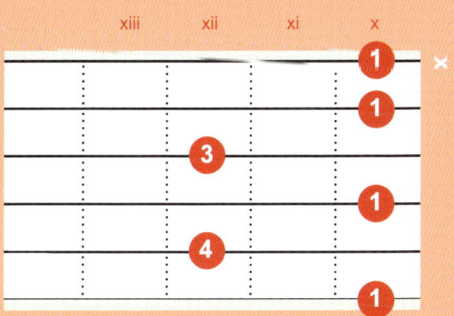

Barre using an A shape with one finger left off, to give you a low 7th on the open string.

LEVEL FOUR

Four positions for C⁷ᵗʰ now.

C⁷ᵗʰ (open)

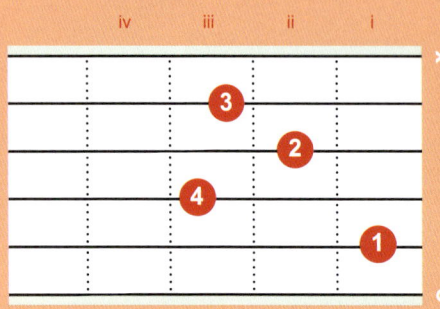

Open—an adaptation of the C you already know.

C⁷ᵗʰ
(barre, low 7th, root on E string)

Barre using an E shape with one finger left off, to give you a low 7th on an open string.

C⁷ᵗʰ

(barre, high 7th, root on E string)

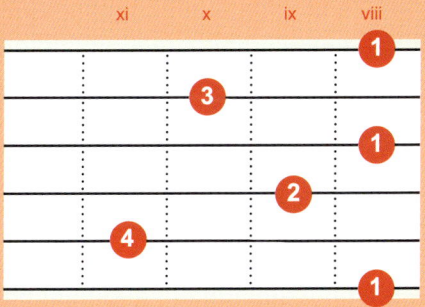

Barre using an E shape with finger 4 added to the top of the chord, to give you a high 7th.

C⁷ᵗʰ

(barre, root on A string)

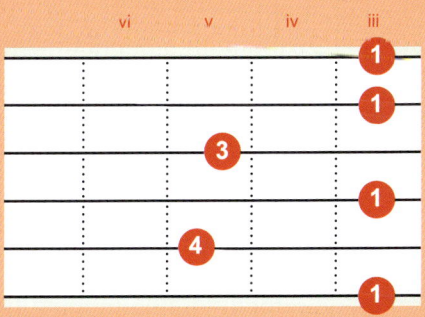

Barre using an A shape with one finger left off, to give you a low 7th on the open string.

LEVEL FOUR

F is always a challenge when learning guitar, as a barre chord on the first fret requires more first-finger pressure than on any other fret.

F⁷ᵗʰ

(barre, low 7th, root on E string)

F⁷ᵗʰ

(barre, high 7th, root on E string)

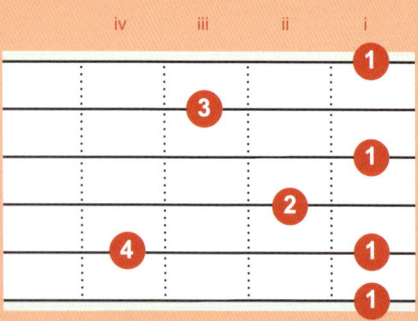

F⁷ᵗʰ

(barre, root on A string)

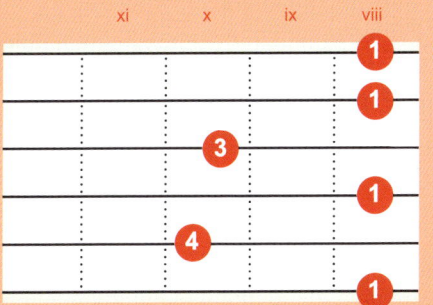

LEVEL FOUR

B⁷ᵗʰ (open)

Open—a chord you know.

B⁷ᵗʰ
(barre, root on A string)

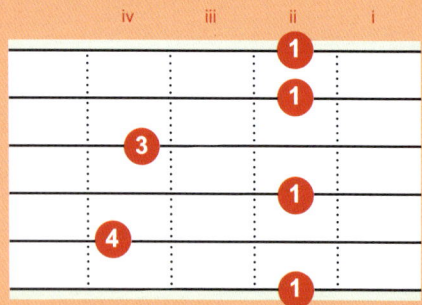

Barre using an A shape.

B⁷ᵗʰ

(barre, low 7th, root on E string)

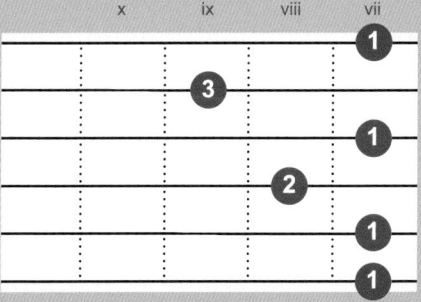

Barre, E shape with low 7th.

B⁷ᵗʰ

(barre, high 7th, root on E string)

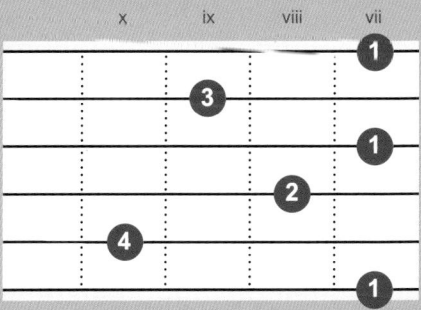

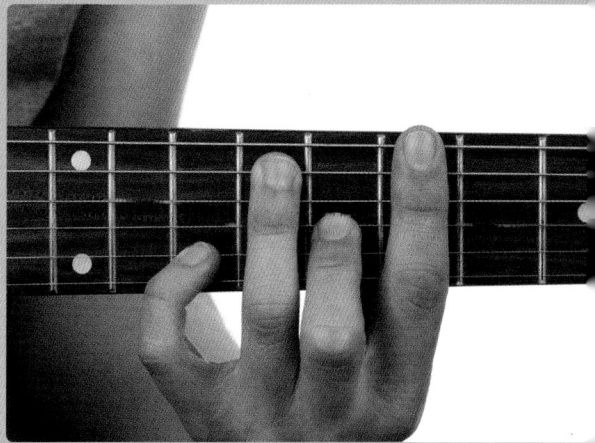

Barre E shape with high 7th.

LEVEL FOUR

MAJOR 7THS

You've already learned a few open versions of Major 7ths (the symbol is a small triangle), which we include here. Now meet the rest of the family—some of them are rather challenging!

You will hear they all share the same jazzy sound, quite different from the 7ths you've just looked at. It's important not to confuse the two.

So get your jazz hat on! Meet the Major 7ths, presented here in a selection of positions—open and barre, and some that look like barre chords, but they're not!

In the keys of **A**, **B**, **C**, **D**, **E**, **F**, and **G**.

A Major⁷ᵗʰ (open)

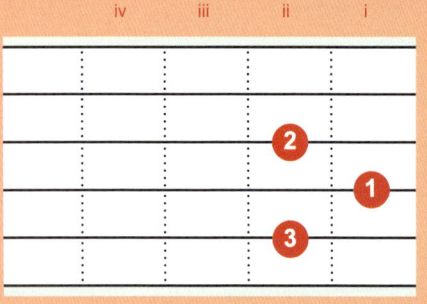

A Major⁷ᵗʰ
(root on E string)

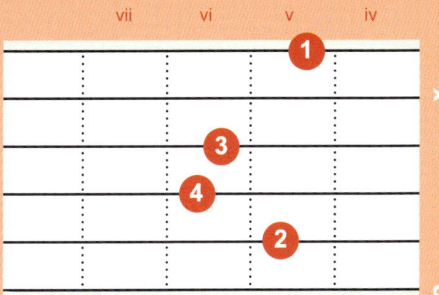

This chord looks a lot like a barre chord version of D minor—but it's not! With that chord you put the A minor directly in front of a barred finger 1. With this shape, you form an A minor shape **directly underneath** your first finger, not in front of it, as you are used to doing.

Finger 1 presses down on the bottom E string only. However, we don't want the A string to sound, so allow your first finger to lightly mute that string.

B Major⁷ᵗʰ

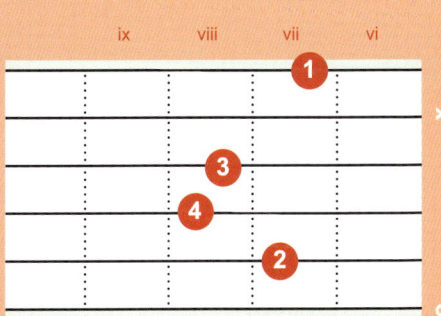

Here's the same shape, built on the seventh fret.

LEVEL FOUR

B Major⁷ᵗʰ
(barre, root on A string)

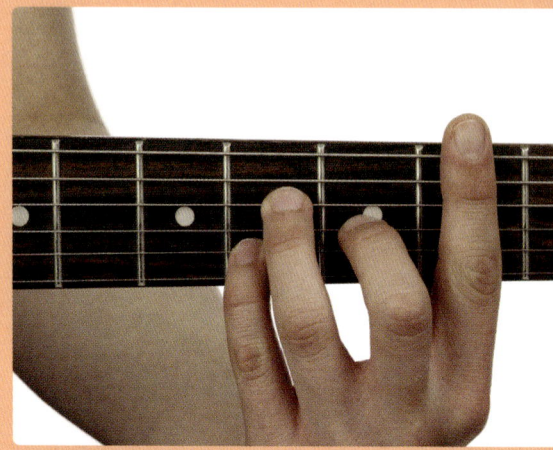

Finger 1 across all the strings in the usual way. Now form an A Major⁷ᵗʰ figure in front of it with your remaining three fingers.

C Major⁷ᵗʰ (open)

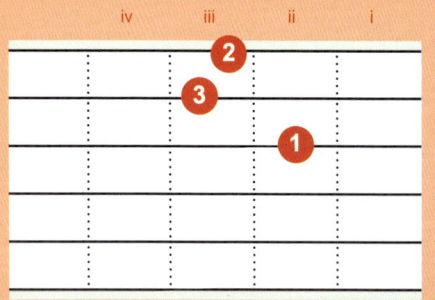

C Major⁷ᵗʰ
(barre, root on A string)

Finger 1 across all the strings in the usual way. Now form an open A Major⁷ᵗʰ figure in front of it with your remaining three fingers.

C Major⁷ᵗʰ
(root on E string)

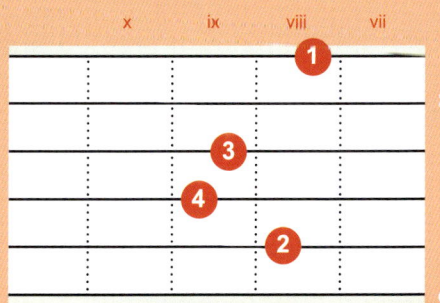

Finger 1 on the bottom E string only (but lightly muting open A string). Form an A minor shape directly underneath.

LEVEL FOUR

D Major⁷ᵗʰ (open)

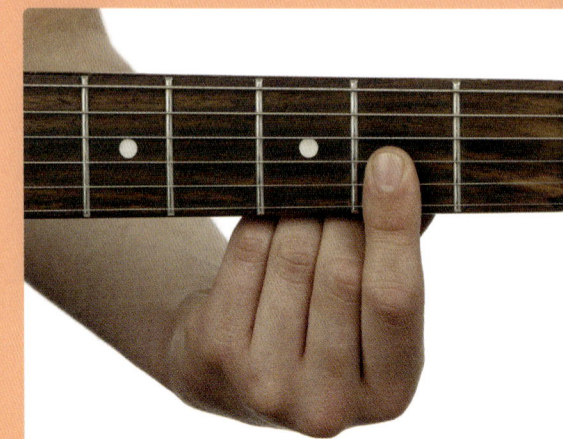

D Major⁷ᵗʰ
(barre, root on A string)

D Major⁷ᵗʰ
(root on E string)

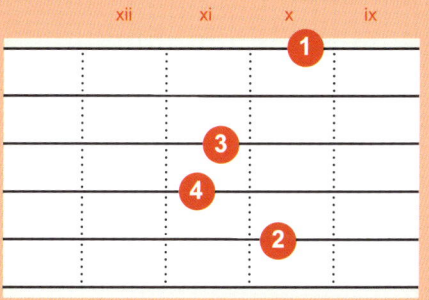

Finger 1 on the bottom E string only (but lightly muting open A string). Form an A minor shape directly underneath.

E Major⁷ᵗʰ (open)

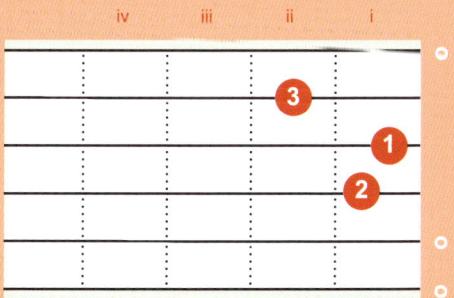

LEVEL FOUR

E Major⁷ᵗʰ
(barre, root on A string)

E Major⁷ᵗʰ
(root on E string)

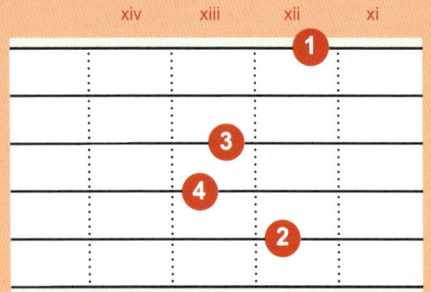
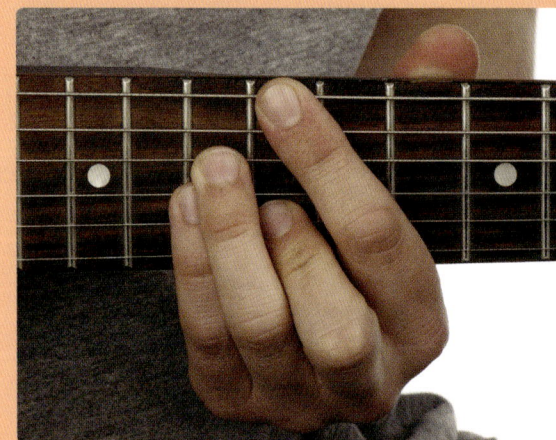

F Major⁷ᵗʰ (open)

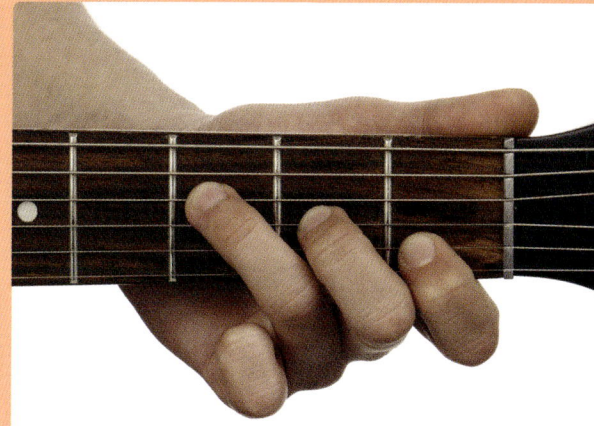

F Major⁷ᵗʰ
(root on E string)

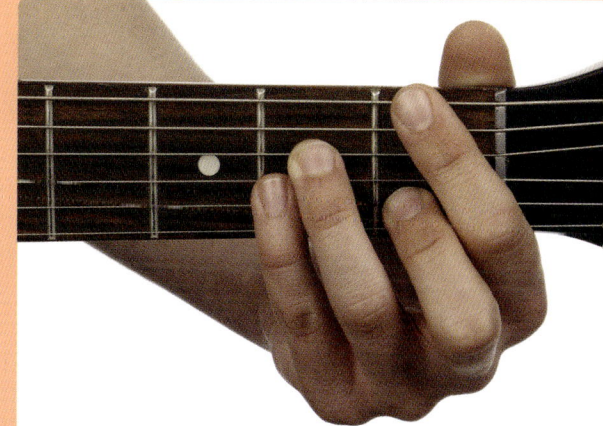

LEVEL FOUR

F Major⁷ᵗʰ
(barre, root on A string)

MINOR 7THS

And so, from Major 7th to minor 7th. A whole different mood. Or as Cole Porter put it:

**"There's no love song finer,
but how strange the change from Major to minor
Every time we say goodbye."**

As with your dominant 7th chords, the seventh note can occur high in the chord, tonally, or an octave lower in the chord, so we'll give you both forms.

And you'll be realizing by now, it may look like a lot of chords, but actually it's the same three or four shapes, in multiple positions, depending on the key you're in. So relax and learn the shapes, identify the different location each time, and you're all over it.

A minor⁷ᵗʰ (open, low 7th)

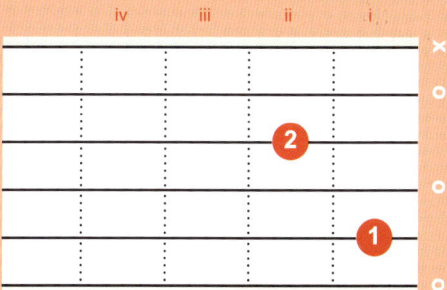
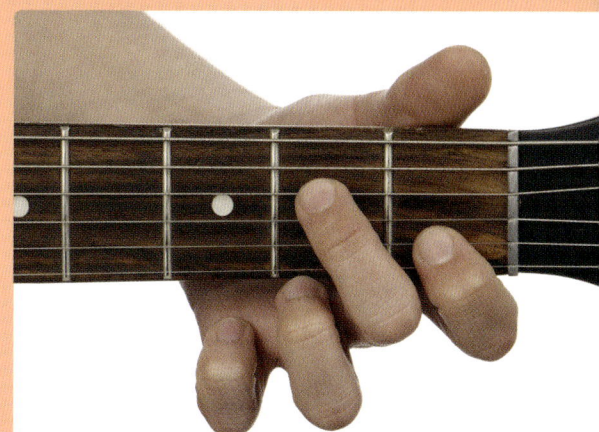

A minor⁷ᵗʰ (open, high 7th)

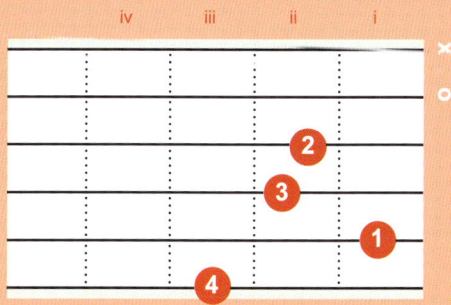

LEVEL FOUR

A minor⁷ᵗʰ (barre, low 7th)

With these barre chords where finger 2 is not involved, use it to reinforce finger 1, as this image demonstrates.

A minor⁷ᵗʰ (barre, high 7th)

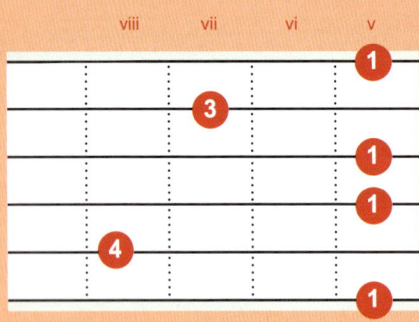

Technically, you could call this a "double 7th," as we haven't "removed" the low 7th. So we have the two 7ths occurring an octave apart within the same chord.

B minor⁷ᵗʰ
(root on A string, low 7th)

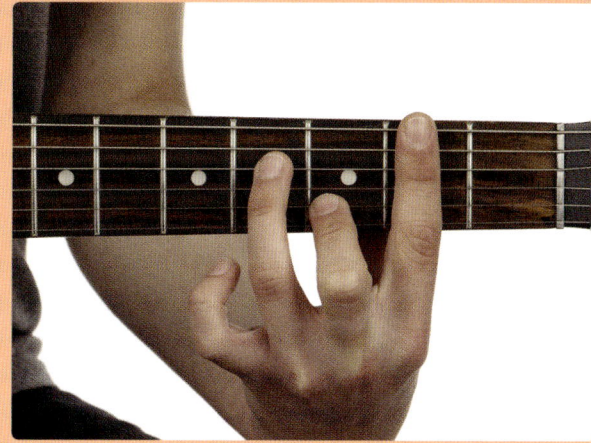

B minor⁷ᵗʰ
(root on A string, high 7th)

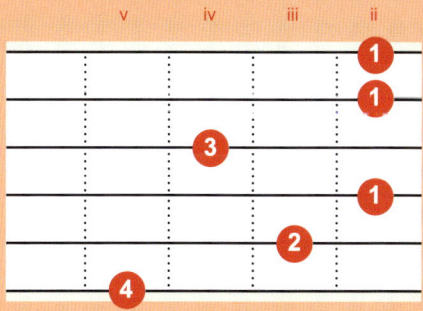

LEVEL FOUR

B minor⁷ᵗʰ
(root on E string, low 7th)

B minor⁷ᵗʰ
(root on E string, high 7th)

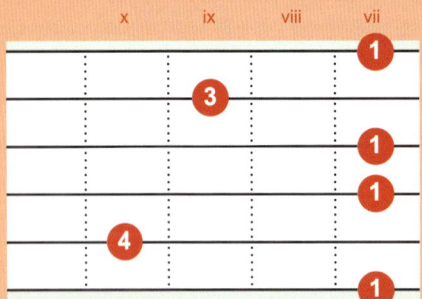

C minor⁷ᵗʰ
(root on A string, low 7th)

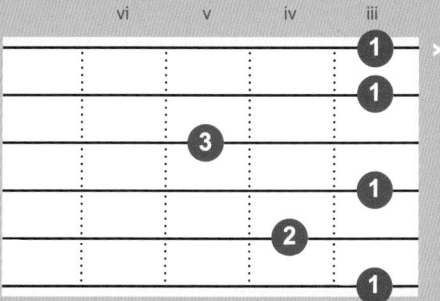

C minor⁷ᵗʰ
(root on A string, high 7th)

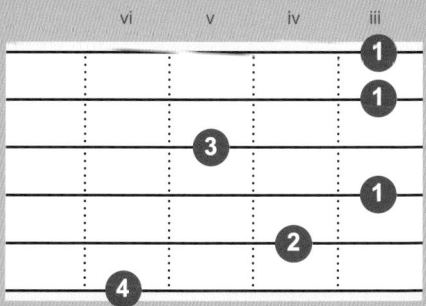

LEVEL FOUR

C minor⁷ᵗʰ
(root on E string, low 7th)

C minor⁷ᵗʰ
(root on E string, high 7th)

D minor⁷ᵗʰ (open)

This is like a baby version of F (top three strings only), with finger 1 covering the top two strings. Strum it from the open D.

D minor⁷ᵗʰ

(root on A string, low 7th)

LEVEL FOUR

D minor⁷ᵗʰ
(root on A string, high 7th)

Form this shape on the fifth fret.

D minor⁷ᵗʰ
(root on E string, low 7th)

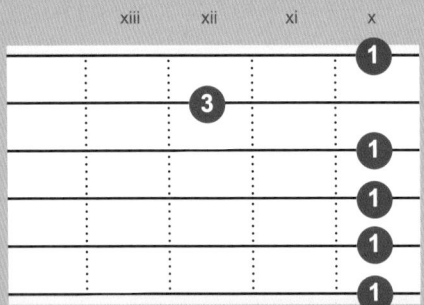

D minor⁷ᵗʰ
(root on E string, high 7th)

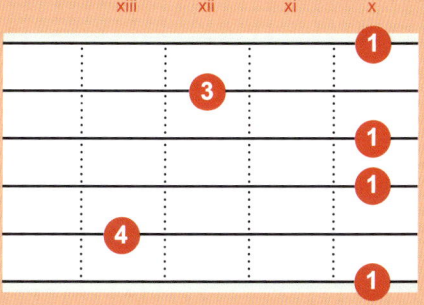

Build this Dᵐ up on the tenth fret. It's effectively a "double seventh"—it has the 7th in both low and high positions.

Many of Joni Mitchell's incomparable songs demonstrate both a jazziness and a wistfulness that each come from her love of Major and minor 7ths.

LEVEL FOUR

E MINOR 7TH

Many versions of the same chord again. But it's all about showing you how to travel around with it. Because when you use the chord, you will be in the middle of a few others somewhere or other, up and down the neck, wanting to sneak a minor 7th in. And if the tempo's fast, you'll need to stay in the same neighborhood!

Let's start with the easiest chord in the world . . .

E minor⁷ᵗʰ (open, low 7th)

Now we'll add the high 7th.

E minor⁷ᵗʰ (open, high 7th)

E minor⁷ᵗʰ (open, double 7th)

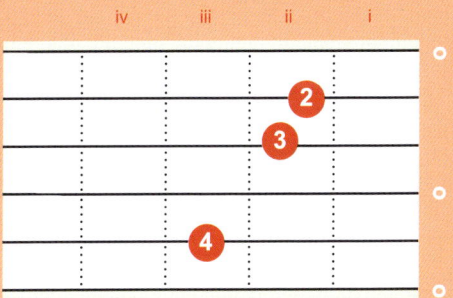

Now we'll "close" the low 7th by making an E minor chord underneath the high 7th.

E minor⁷ᵗʰ
(root on A string, low 7th)

LEVEL FOUR

E minor⁷ᵗʰ
(root on A string, high 7th)

F minor⁷ᵗʰ
(root on E string, low 7th)

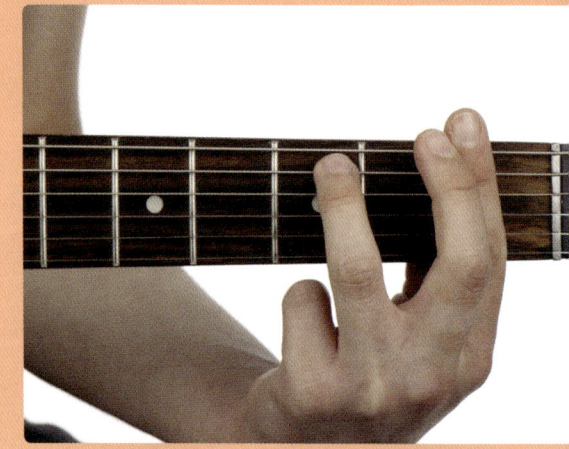

F minor⁷ᵗʰ
(root on E string, high 7th)

F minor⁷ᵗʰ
(root on A string, low 7th)

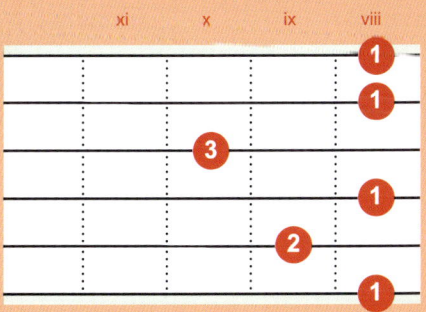
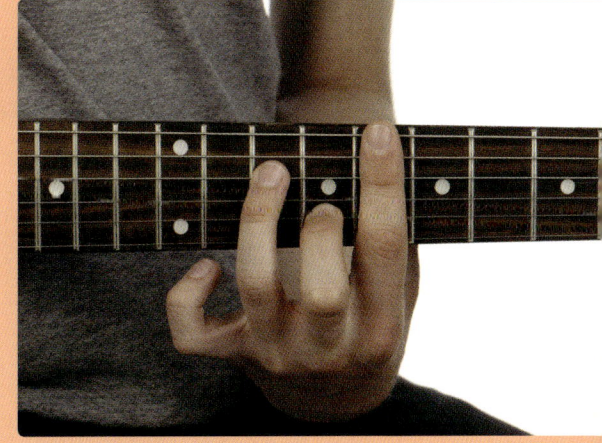

LEVEL FOUR

F minor⁷ᵗʰ
(root on A string, high 7th)

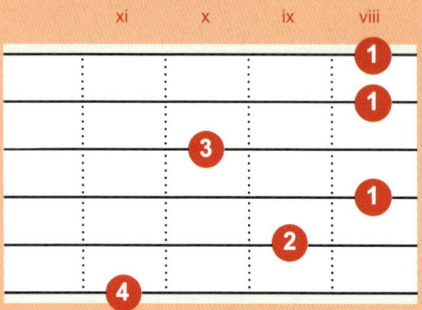

G minor⁷ᵗʰ
(root on E string, low 7th)

G minor⁷ᵗʰ
(root on E string, high 7th)

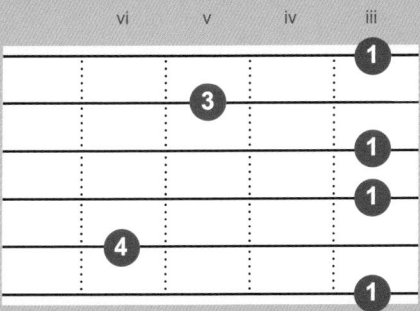

G minor⁷ᵗʰ
(root on A string, low 7th)

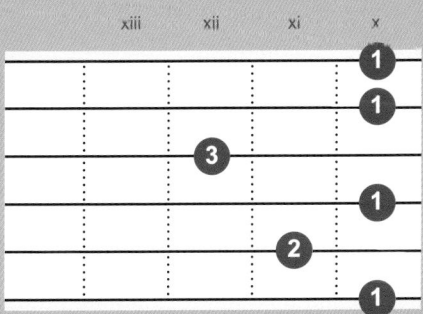

LEVEL FOUR

G minor⁷ᵗʰ

(root on A string, high 7th)

SUS 4THS

Musicians talk of sus 4s, which is short for **suspended fourths** (which no one ever calls them!).

You are well aware by now that your basic chord is a three-note affair made up of the first, third, and fifth note of the scale. Sus 4s occur when we temporarily replace the third in the chord with a fourth—a note one semitone higher. The way we do this is by putting our finger on the same string, one fret up from the finger playing the third, which usually we don't remove. So now you have two fingers on the same string. The finger one fret above the other ensures we don't hear the note a fret below it.

You can see how that looks opposite, as we take the chord of A Major and turn it into a sus 4.

A sus⁴

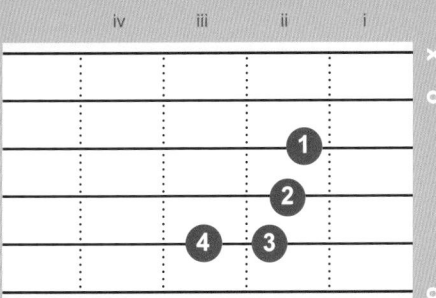
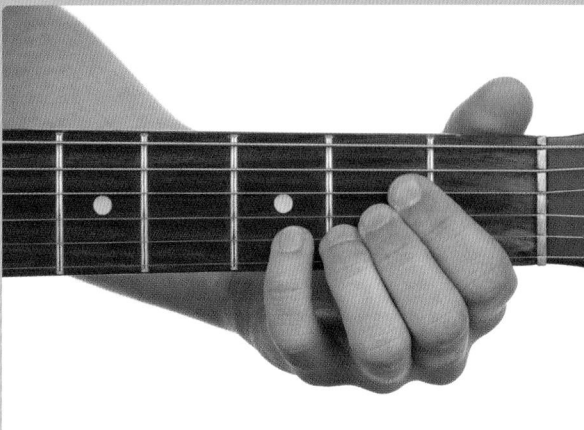

As soon as we remove finger 4, finger 3's note will sound on the next strum. Try strumming three sus 4s, then removing finger 4 for the fourth strum and hold the chord, to ring for the next bar. Like this:

1	2	3	4		1	2	3	4
A sus4	A sus4	A sus4	A	-				

Let's do the same with a D sus4—the "sus" occurs on the top E string this time.

D sus⁴

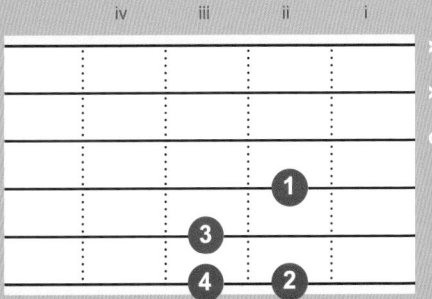

117

LEVEL FOUR

Strum three sus 4s, removing finger 4 on fourth strum and hold the chord for the next bar:

1	2	3	4		1	2	3	4
Dsus4	Dsus4	Dsus4	D	-				

And again, with E. The sus occurs on the D string:

E sus⁴

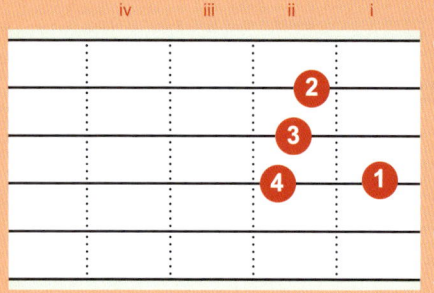

1	2	3	4		1	2	3	4
Esus4	Esus4	Esus4	E	-				

Now let's combine those sequences into one:

1	2	3	4		1	2	3	4
Asus4	Asus4	Asus4	A	-				
1	2	3	4		1	2	3	4
Dsus4	Dsus4	Dsus4	D	-				
1	2	3	4		1	2	3	4
Esus4	Esus4	Esus4	E	-				
1	2	3	4		1	2	3	4
Asus4	Asus4	Asus4	A	-				

CAGED **CHORDS**

This is an acronym, of course. And it's a chord system widely recognized by guitarists, giving you different options for shaping your chord all along the fretboard. This is incredibly useful toward knowing which notes to select when playing a guitar solo.

The CAGED system is a barre chord set-up consisting of five shapes, taking you up and down the neck in distinct zones, using the open Major chords C, A, G, E, and D.

Here's how it works. When you play an open C, you can then re-create the chord moving up the neck (toward the body) in intervals, using the letters of CAGED—in that order.

So: play an open C.

SHAPE ONE:
OPEN C

LEVEL FOUR

SHAPE TWO:
C WITH CAGED A

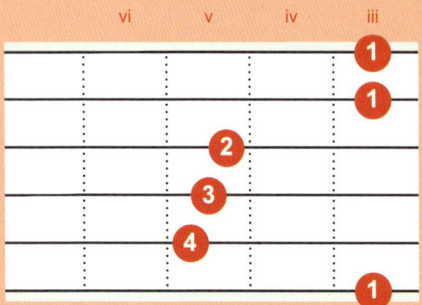

How many frets up the neck did open C extend? To the third fret. Okay, now make a barre with finger 1 on that third fret and with your remaining fingers put an A in front of it. Can you hear? It's also a C.

SHAPE THREE:
C WITH CAGED G

How many frets up the neck does that chord extend? To the fifth fret. So, now make a barre with finger 1 on that fifth fret. What's the next letter in our CAGED acronym? We've used up the C and A, so an open G next. It's a bit of a stretch, one of those chords you need to practice by taking your hand off the fretboard and putting it back on a few times.

SHAPE FOUR:
C WITH CAGED E

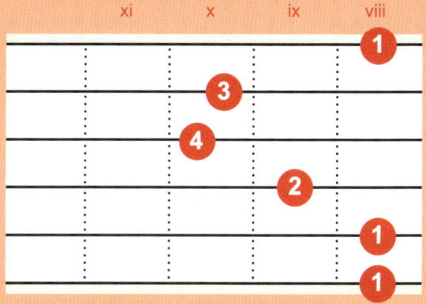

That chord extended to the eighth fret.

Finger 1 on eighth fret. E Major in front of it. It's an "oh, yeah!" moment, isn't it? You've got this now.

SHAPE FIVE:
C WITH CAGED D

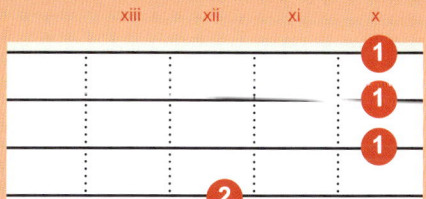

That chord extended to the tenth fret.

Finger 1 on tenth fret. The last of our CAGED letters now, the D. It's a barre chord, of course (and a tricky one), but strum it from the A string.

LEVEL FOUR

Exactly the same five-shape process can be applied to each of the letters in our CAGED acronym, giving you five different versions of that chord, moving up the fretboard.

Try it with the next letter we come to: the A. Our acronym becomes AGEDC now. Follow exactly the same process:

SHAPE 1: Play an open A Major.

Check out which fret that chord extends to (the second).

SHAPE 2: Finger 1 barred across that fret.

Next letter is a G, so form an open G above it (quite a stretch!).

Check out which fret that chord extends to (the fifth).

SHAPE 3: Finger 1 barred across that fret.

Next letter is an E, so form an open E above it.

SHAPE 4: The last chord extended to the seventh fret and the next letter is a D, so barre across the seventh and form a D.

SHAPE 5: The last shape, you need to barre across the ninth and make a C, instead of the tenth, so it breaks the rule. There's always one! But you can cope with it, because . . .

YEP—YOU'RE A ZEP!

Right: Robert Plant was Led Zeppelin's lead singer

LEVEL FOUR

PENTATONIC SCALE

The scales you have learned so far in this book have been your regular Major scales with seven notes in the octave (okay, they had eight notes, but the eighth note was the same as the first, an octave up and therefore not part of the same octave).

Now it's time to meet the pentatonic scale format, the basis for all the great guitar solos!

As the name would suggest, it has five notes in the scale—the first, second, third, fifth, and sixth notes of the regular Major scale. It knocks out the fourth and seventh notes: the two half-steps or semitones.

The Major scale of C, for instance, goes:

C D E F G A B (C)

The pentatonic Major scale of C, therefore, goes:

C D E G A (C)

We start with the scale of A Major. On the guitar, the notes of the pentatonic scale occur at either two-fret or three-fret intervals, and in this position are best played by "rocking" between the first and third finger if it's a two-fret interval, or the first and fourth finger if it's the wider, three-fret interval. To help guide you, the tabs here include small numbers at the bottom of the tab showing you which finger to use for each note.

To stretch your fretboard journey further, here's the "double pentatonic" of that scale, i.e., one right after another, continuing on up the strings. The stickers will be really useful here.

PENTATONIC SCALE: A Major

1st A – 2nd B – 3rd C# – 4th E – 5th F#

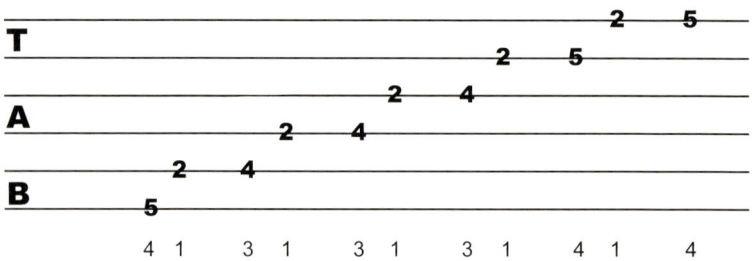

There are twelve Major and twelve minor pentatonic scales and they can be played in five different positions on the fretboard. Too many to show here! But once you get used to the construct of the pentatonic and decide where you want the starting note to be, you can soon figure out these scales for yourself.

Minor pentatonic scales feature later in the book. Here's another double pentatonic Major scale, this one incorporating open string notes, making it ridiculously easy to play.

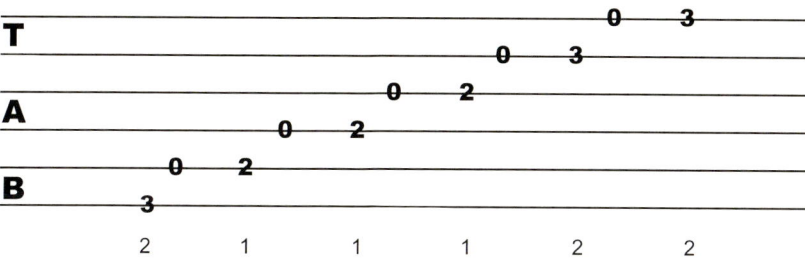

3 STEPS FORWARD, ONE STEP BACK

A great way to practice these scales is to play the first three notes, then go back one note and do the next three, progressing all the way to the top note.

PENTATONIC EXERCISE: G Major

1st G – 2nd A – 3rd B – 4th D – 5th E

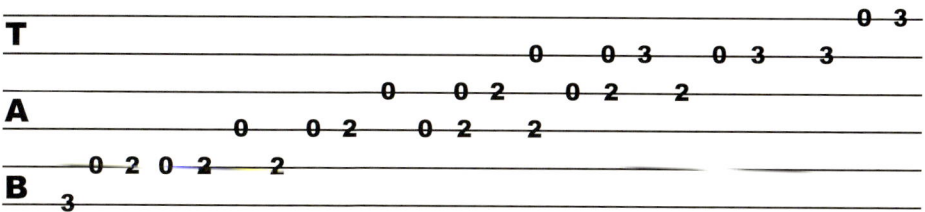

Then reverse the process all the way back:

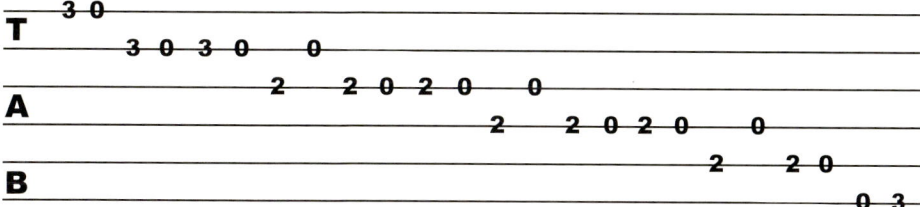

LEVEL FOUR

RIFF REWARD (ZEP)

Congratulations, you've earned a Riff Reward! Not a riff as such this time, but a collection of customized chords adapted from orthodox shapes.

"Wonderwall," a Noel Gallagher song (in which he compares his girlfriend to a schoolboy poster wall of pop stars and soccer stars) was the biggest selling single in the USA for his band, Oasis. The song spawned these variations on four well-known chords, and they have since gone on to be adopted by many other artists while songwriting.

Each of the chords has fingers 3 and 4 locked in the same position on the top two strings. They are unmoving, while fingers 1 and 2 make all the moves. They are open-chord, customized versions of E minor, G Major, D Major, and A Major.

Play it with your capo across the second fret and strum it **down, down, up up down down**.

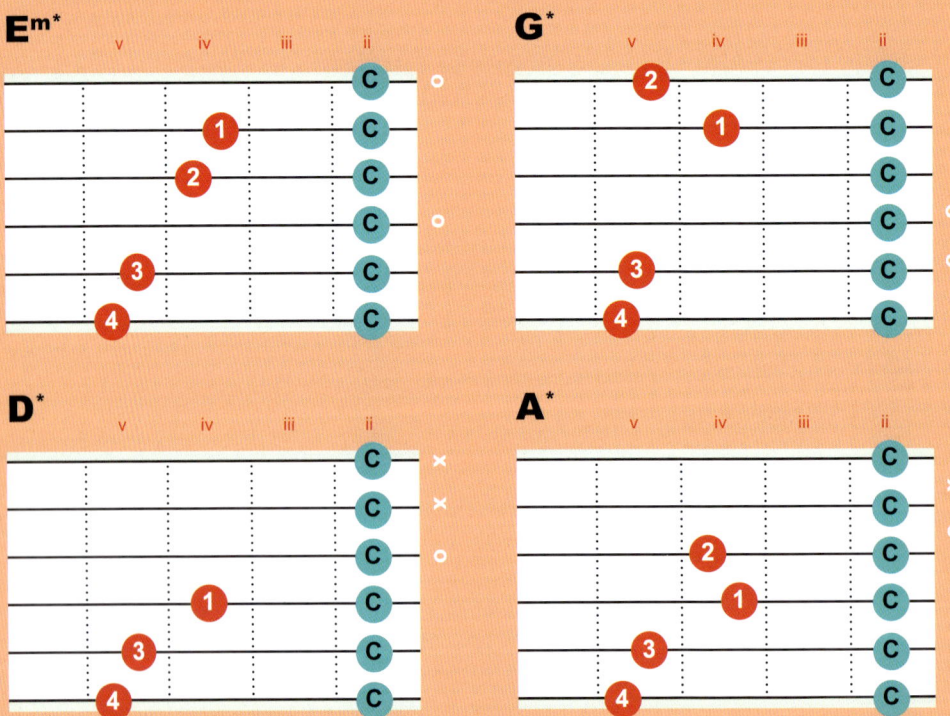

Right: Noel Gallagher, lead guitarist and co-lead singer of Oasis

LEVEL FIVE: MUSE

In this final level, we will introduce you to a further forty-five chords: diminished, augmented, Major 6ths, minor 6ths, dominant 9ths, and minor 9ths. You'll meet more scales: minor, blues, and double pentatonics. You'll also get to understand the twelve-bar blues, and we'll unravel the mysteries of the circle of fifths.

Frontman Matt Bellamy has introduced all the elements of classical music into the gene pool of rock 'n' roll to create a higher level of musicianship. Muse have set the bar high!

Left: Muse lead singer and lead guitarist, Matt Bellamy

LEVEL FIVE

BUSIER FINGERPICKING

While this book is primarily about chords and, therefore, the fretboard hand that forms those shapes, the other hand that plays the strings cannot be completely ignored. I would like to pay further attention now to arpeggiating your chord, or, as it is more commonly known, fingerpicking.

In **Level Three**, you plucked your way through the verse of "Hallelujah," using the thumb and index finger of your strumming hand. Now we are going to incorporate the middle finger, too, and vary the pattern a little, involving a few more chords.

This sounds a whole lot like "Hotel California," but this is not exactly how The Eagles played it. However, this will work very well alongside it.

Don Henley said, "We were in pursuit of a note-perfect song." Primary composer Don Felder came up with the basic chords while playing on the beach, and its chimingly resonant fingerpicked intro is perfectly suited to our purposes, as we work to improve our fingerstyle.

Here's the chord sequence:

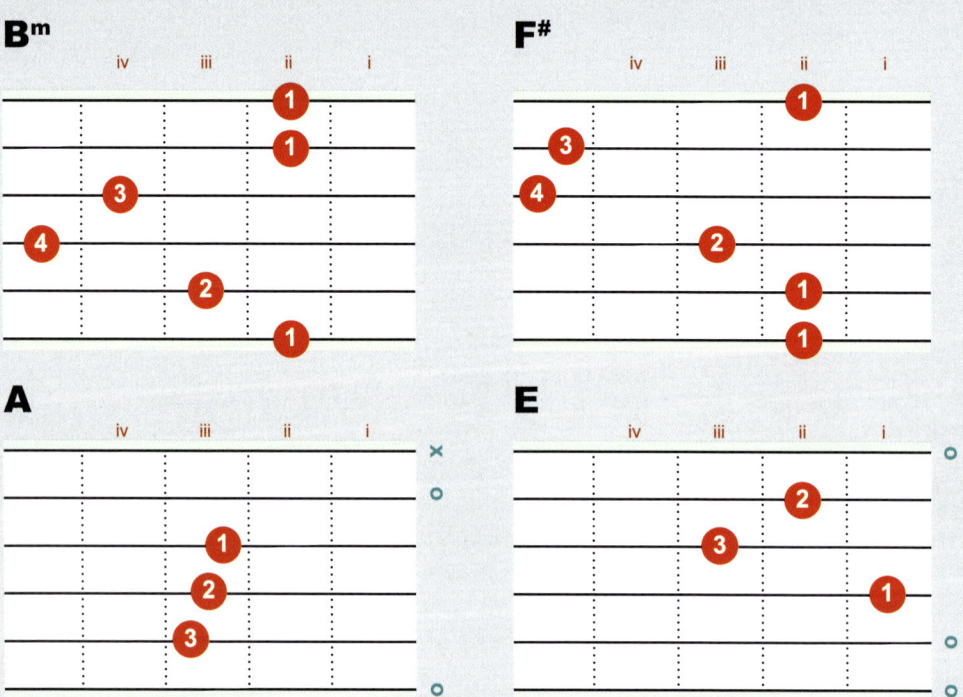

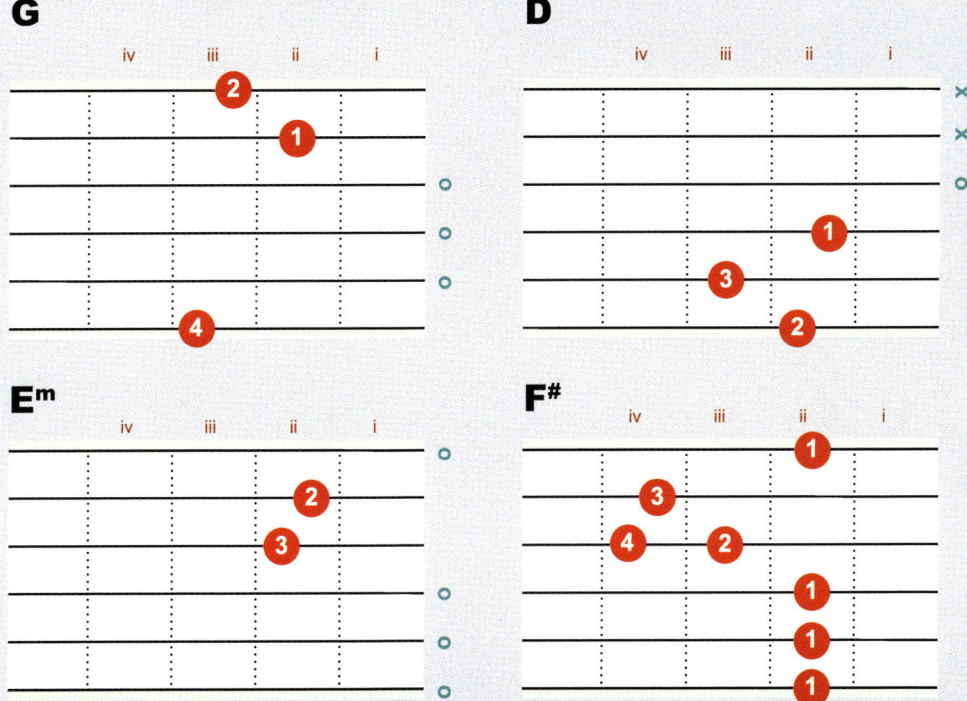

Here is the fingerpicking pattern. The letters refer to your strings:

Root B G E, B G E

Each chord will be plucked from the root note of that chord, followed by the top three strings, in the above order. So, the root note will vary according to the chord, but the rest remain constant.

- Your thumb will pluck the root note and the G string, with a downstroke motion (toward the floor).
- Your index finger (finger 1) will play the B string, with an upstroke motion (toward the thumb).
- Your middle finger (finger 2) will be responsible for the E string, with an upstroke.
- So, applying our fingerpicking pattern to the "Hotel California" chords, here is that sequence, in tab form. Each chord tab lasts for two bars. After the last note has been plucked, count 2, 3, 4 (to get you to the end of the second bar) before commencing with the next tab.

LEVEL FIVE

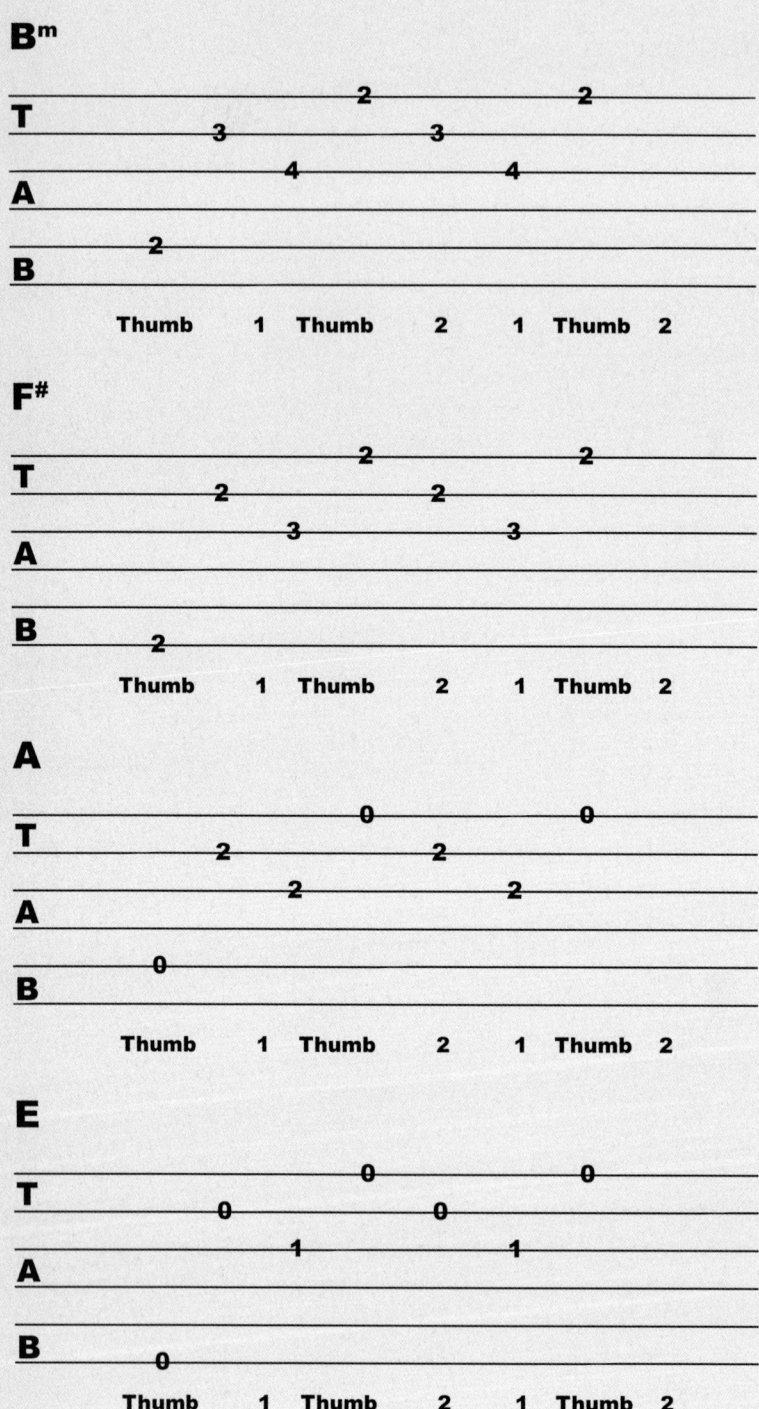

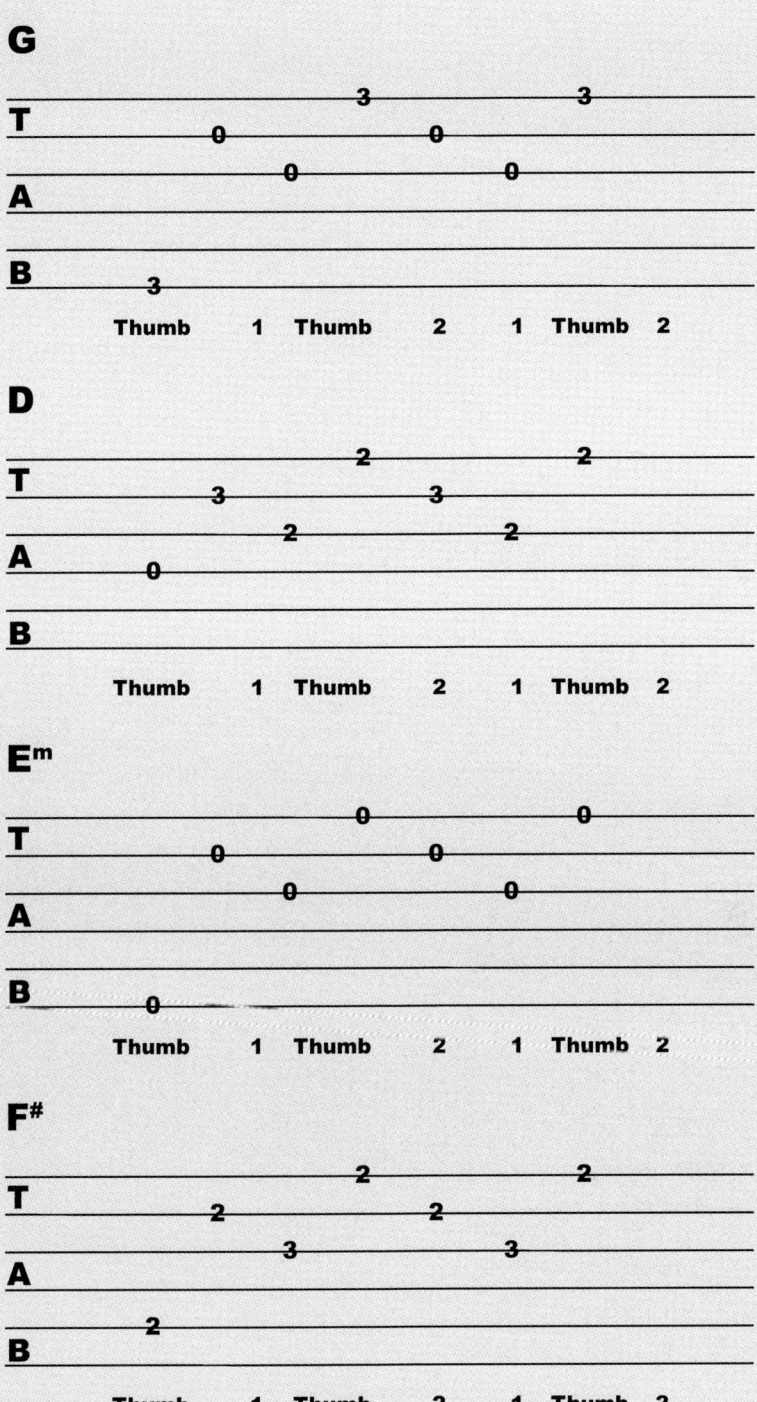

LEVEL FIVE

TWO **CARTOON CHORDS**

Meet Diminished and Augmented. These crazy heavyweights would grace any chord sequence with their resonant beauty, but they do behave in a rather strange way . . .

DIMINISHED

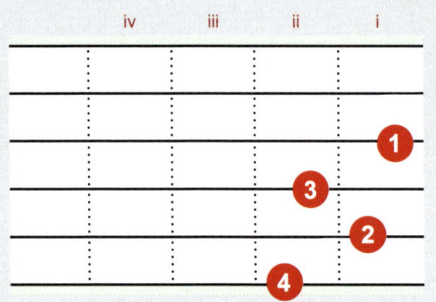

Have you mastered it? Move it up the guitar neck by three frets and play it again. See? Same chord. Now play another three—same chord. And another three. When you've got the hang of it, try it quickly: first fret, fourth, seventh, tenth. It sounds like a cartoon tune!

This chord has three positions. It can be built on any of the first three frets—it all depends on the key you're in. Repeat every three frets, all the way up until you run out of road.

AUGMENTED

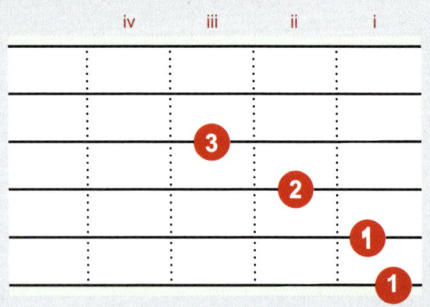

Got it? Now move it up the guitar neck by four frets and play it again. Same chord. Now another four—same chord. And another four. Now try it quickly: first fret, fifth, ninth.

This chord has four positions. It can be built on any of the first four frets, depending on the key you're in. And, knowing it repeats, you can build it higher or lower on the fretboard, depending on where you're playing the group of chords around it at the time.

MORE CHORD FAMILIES: MAJOR 6th

A^M6 (open)

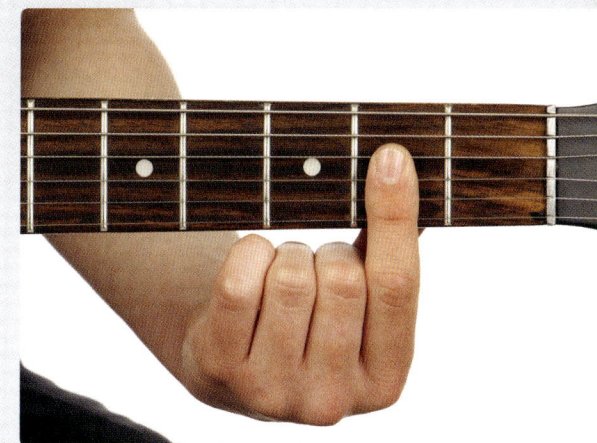

A^M6 (barre)

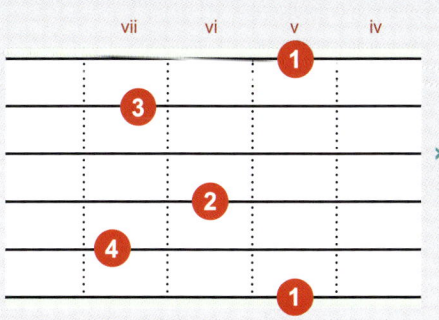

With the barre version of the Major 6th chord, you need to mute the D string. This is done by slightly "leaning over" with finger 3 so that it lightly rests on the string below—the D.

LEVEL FIVE

B^M6 (root on A string)

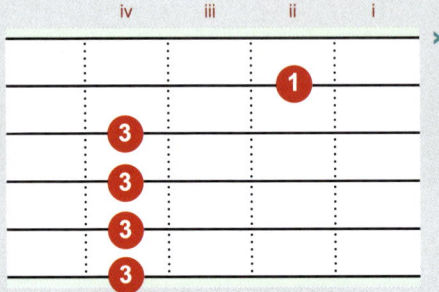

B^M6 (barre)

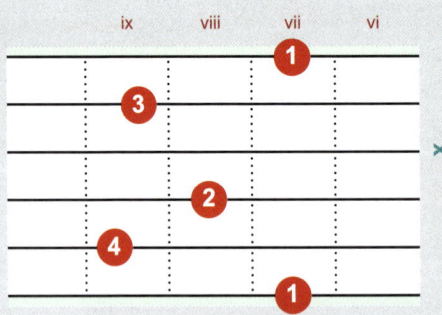

C^M6 (open)

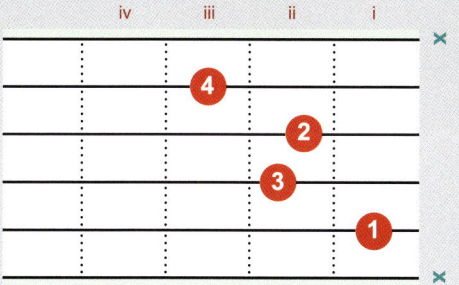
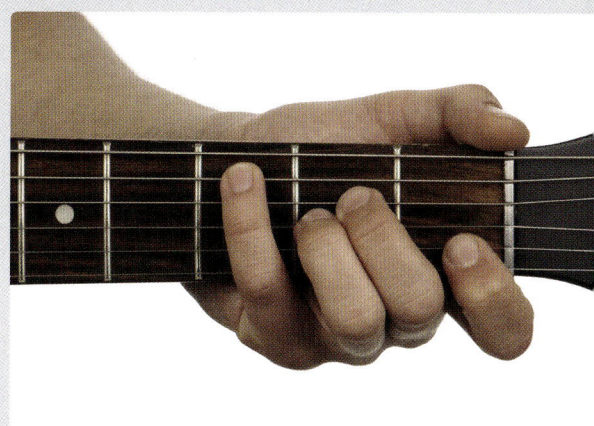

C^M6 (barre)

LEVEL FIVE

D^{M6} (open)

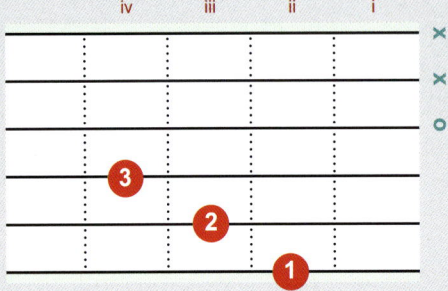
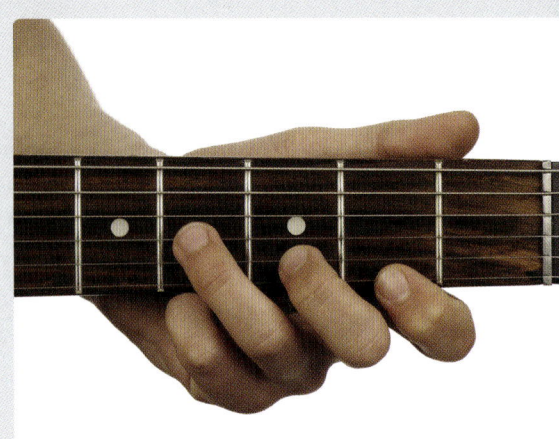

D^{M6} (root on A string)

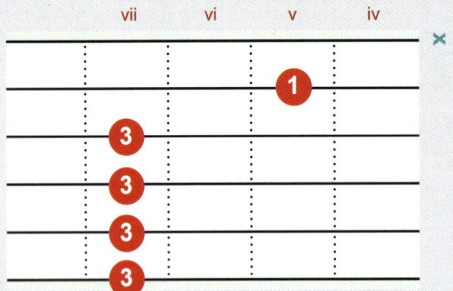

The open E Major 6th demonstrates so clearly how all these chords are just like all your dominant 7ths—the added 6th note is just a semitone lower down than the high 7th was. So, whereas with E7 finger 4 played B string fret 3, now it tucks in under your E Major shape on B2.

E^{M6} (open)

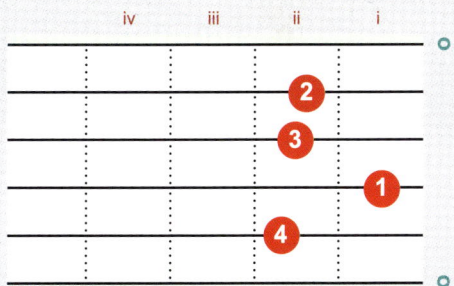

E^{M6} (root on A string)

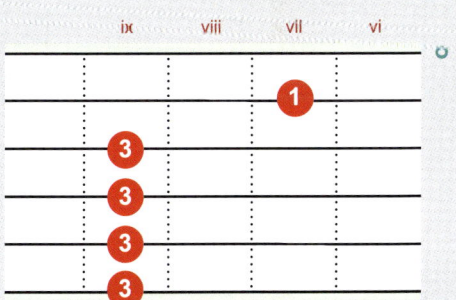

LEVEL FIVE

F^{M6} (open)

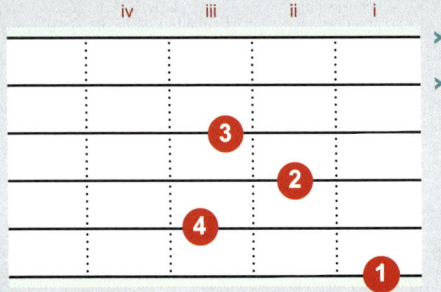

F^{M6} (barre)

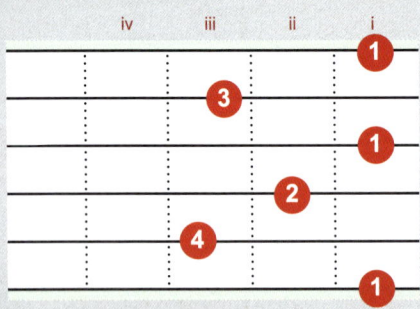

Try strumming 4 in the bar on an F Major barre chord, adding the 6th on strum 3. Then (keep strumming), wiggle finger 1 up one fret to the 7th position and back down to the 6th. Hey, you're playing the blues!

You've met this one before, but it's another chord that perfectly demonstrates the "semitone down" difference between a 6th and a 7th. This is G7 without the first finger covering E string fret 1.

G^{M6} (open)

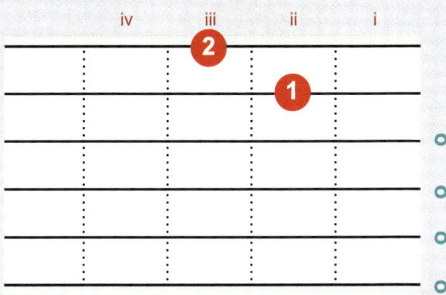

G^{M6} (barre)

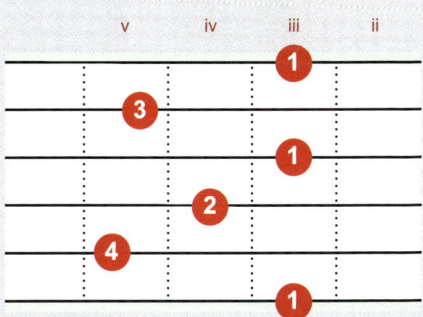

LEVEL FIVE

NATURAL **MINOR SCALE**

There is more than one type of minor scale. The "natural" is the most common. Here it is:

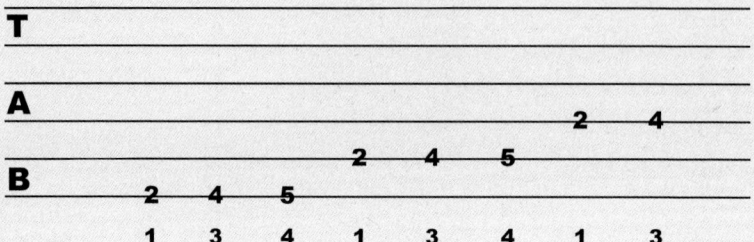

Remember, the small numbers running along the bottom indicate which finger to use.

Get used to the shape. Played this way, the scale always starts on the E string and can be moved to a variety of starting notes on that string, to give you a minor scale in different keys.

Played from the second fret, for instance (as illustrated above), it is the scale of F#, as the note of the E string on the second fret is F#. Whatever note the scale starts on, that's the key it's in.

Played from the third fret, the starting note on the E string is a G. So now that same shape delivers the G natural minor scale:

G natural minor

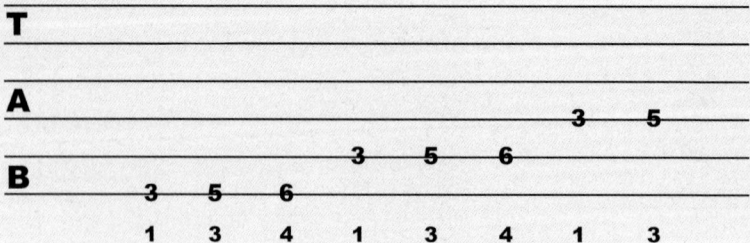

Played from the fifth fret, the starting note on the E string is an A.
So now that same shape gives you an **A minor scale**:

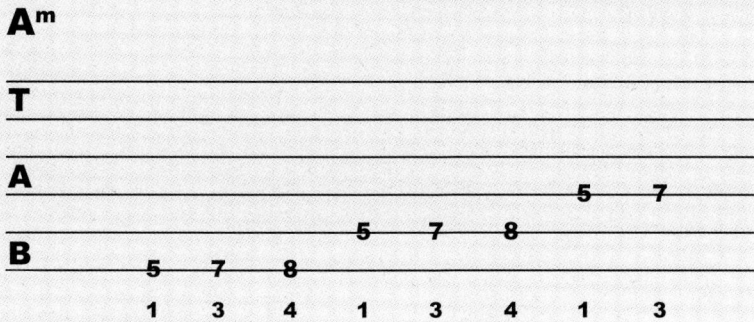

Starting on the eighth fret, it becomes a **C minor scale**:

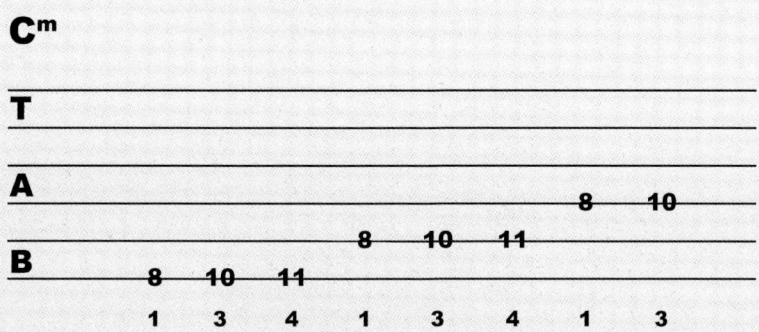

MINOR 6TH CHORDS

There are many choices when it comes to shaping a chord—up to six different hand positions. Here, we offer three: open versions of a minor chord, the barre version with the root on the E string, and something very similar to the barre version with the root on the A string. So, templates with which you are already familiar, but adapted now to include the sixth note of the Major scale, threading another color into the melancholy poetry of the minor chord.

(Note: Major 6ths in abbreviation have a capital M and minor 6ths a lowercase one.)

LEVEL FIVE

A^{m6} (open)

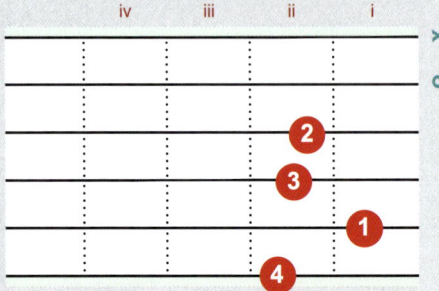

A^{m6} (root on E string)

The barre chord version is an E minor shape against finger 1, using your second and third fingers this time to form the E minor, allowing the freed-up finger 4 to play the extra note, the sixth.

B^m6 (root on A string)

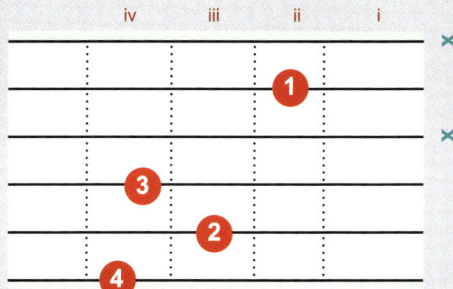

For all intents and purposes, this B^m6 is a barre chord with the root on the A, but with this shape, you don't actually need to barre finger 1 right across the six strings. Just play the note on the A string in a more raised position, yet let your finger lightly impinge on the D string below, so as to mute it.

B^m6 (root on E string)

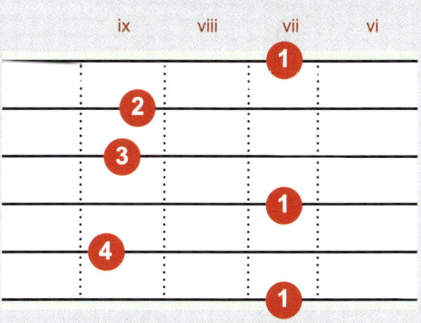

This is the A^m6 with the root on the E you just learned, but two frets further up—the same E minor shape against barred finger 1, using your second and third fingers to form the E^m, with finger 4 on the sixth.

LEVEL FIVE

C^{m6} (root on A string)

One fret further up now, with these two shapes, and you've got the C minor 6th covered.

C^{m6} (root on E string)

Dᵐ⁶ (open)

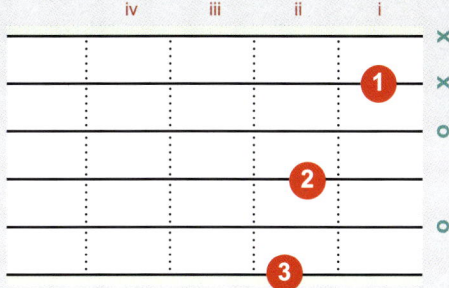

It's D⁷ (or upside-down triangle) without the seventh!

Dᵐ⁶ (root on A string)

LEVEL FIVE

E^{m6} (open)

You can let the bottom E ring out on this one . . .

E^{m6} (root on A string)

F^{m6} (root on E string)

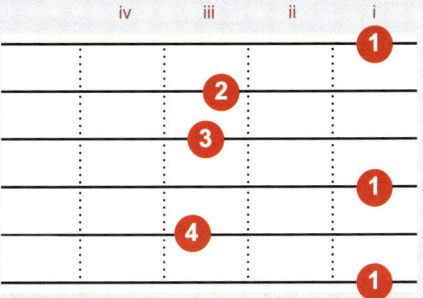
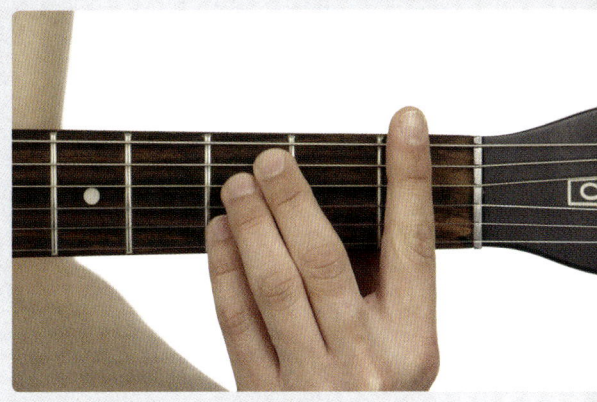

F^{m6} (root on A string)

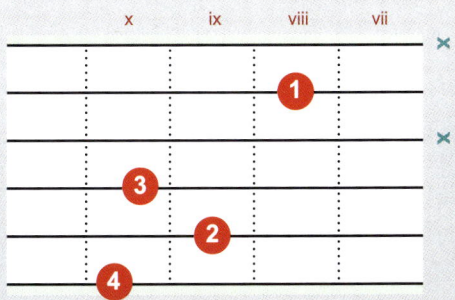

G^{m6} (root on E string)

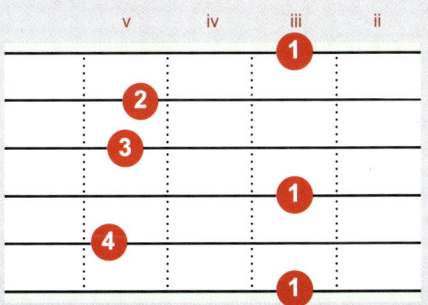
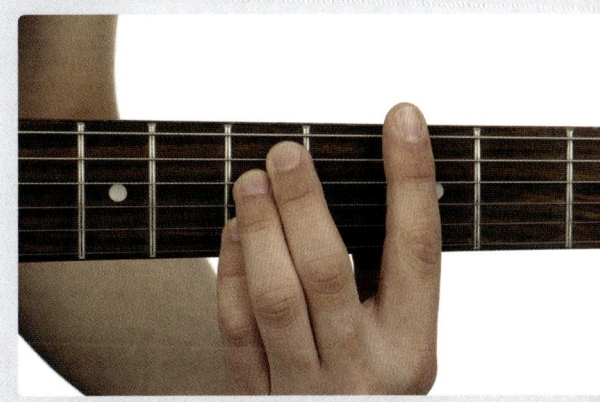

LEVEL FIVE

DOMINANT 9TH

Nobody actually calls this a dominant 9th—it's just a 9th, and what a great little chord it is! Much used in jazz, funk, and blues, it's one of those shapes that you can move anywhere on the fretboard. Played on the third fret as it is here, this is a C^9, as the note on the A string is a C.

C^9

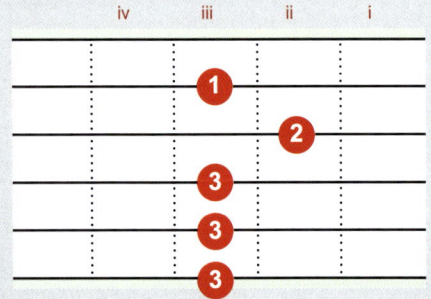

E^9

Here it is in the E position (so you can let the bottom E ring out on this one).

It sounds cool against the open E string, doesn't it?

Now, let's get funky. You're going to play the same chord, but slide up from the fret below. So form the chord on the sixth fret, hit it hard with your playing hand, and immediately slide up to the seventh fret, into the E^9 position. Then mute your strings immediately with your playing hand.

Try doing the same thing, but sliding down from the fret above this time. Form the chord on the eighth fret, swipe it with your playing hand, slide down into the E^9 position, and immediately mute.

Here's a chord sequence:

1	AND	2	AND	3	AND	4	AND		1
		E^9	E^{b9}	E^9		$F^{\#9}$	F^9	-	E^9

In other words, strum your shape on the seventh fret, sixth fret, and back to the seventh fret. Now, play it on the ninth, eighth, and back to the seventh fret.

Try it twice in succession:

1	AND	2	AND	3	AND	4	AND		1	AND	2	AND	3	AND	4	AND		1
		E^9	E^{b9}	E^9		$F^{\#9}$	F^9	-	E^9		E^9	E^{b9}	E^9		$F^{\#9}$	F^9	-	E^9

It goes round and round, while the lead guitar plays the riff:

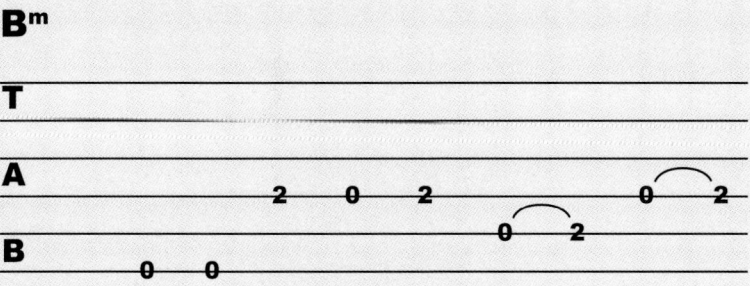

The tab symbol you see here (⌒) represents a hammer-on, a common lead guitar technique. Pluck the open A string and immediately bring your finger down hard on the second fret without plucking the string again. That's a hammer-on.

LEVEL FIVE

MINOR 9TH CHORDS

Here are two patterns for the minor 9th to get used to—one with the root note of the chord on the A string, the other the barre version, root on the E string.

A^{m9} (root on A string)

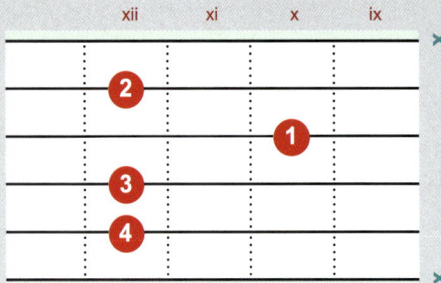

A^{m9} (root on E string)

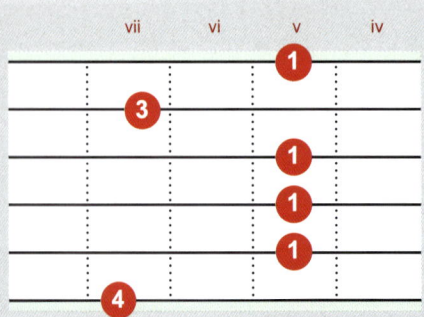

B^{m9} (root on A string)

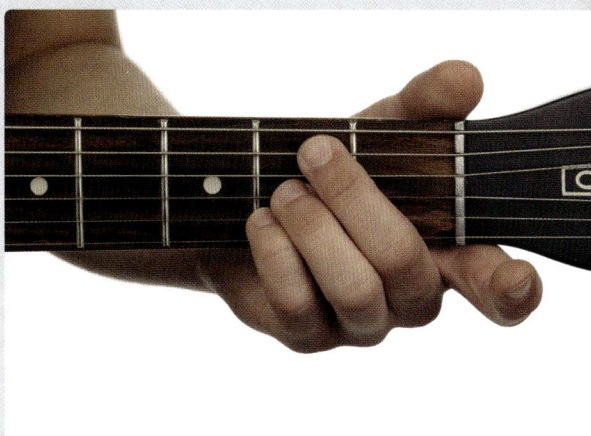

Because of its position, there is no need to fret with your second finger with this one. The required note on the D string is an open D.

B^{m9} (root on E string)

LEVEL FIVE

C^{m9} (root on A string)

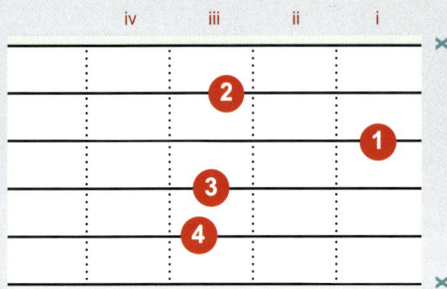

C^{m9} (root on E string)

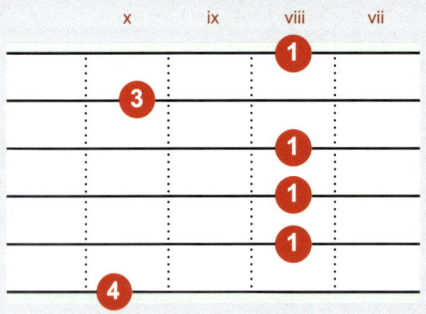

D^m9 (root on A string)

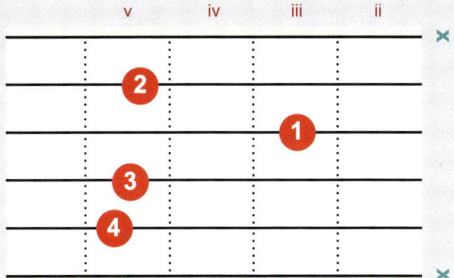

D^m9 (root on E string)

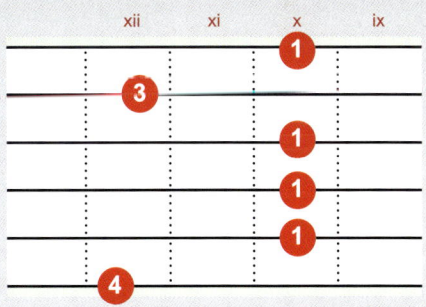
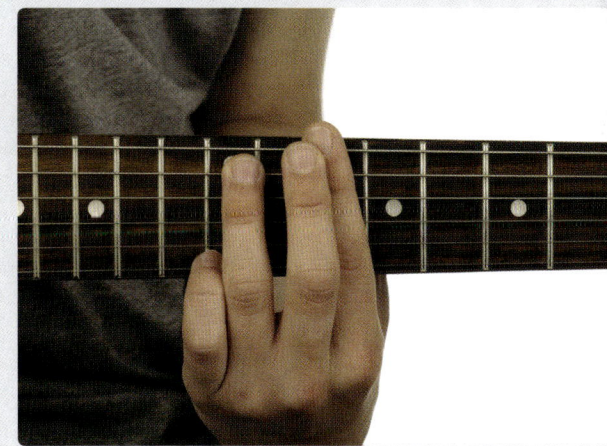

LEVEL FIVE

E^{m9} (root on A string)

Because this is an E chord, you can allow both the open bottom and top E strings to ring.

E^{m9} (root on E string)

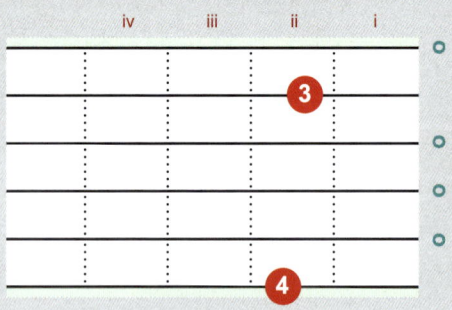

No need to barre for this one.

F^m9 (root on A string)

F^m9 (root on E string)

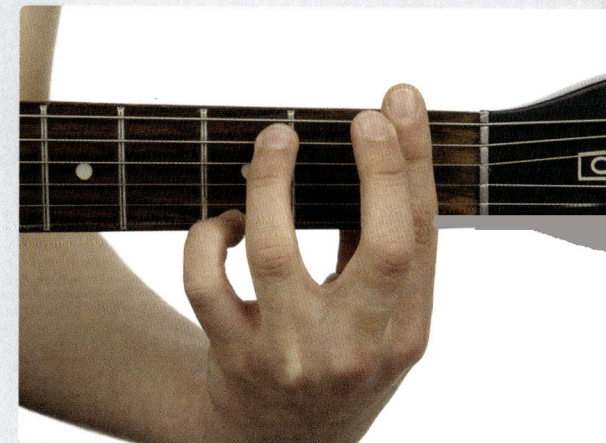

LEVEL FIVE

G^{m9} (root on A string)

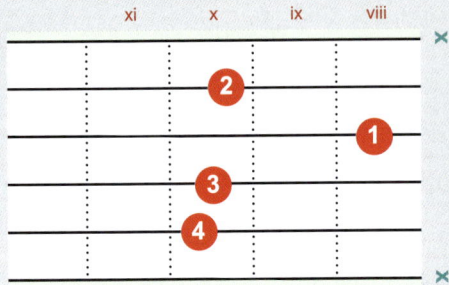

G^{m9} (root on E string)

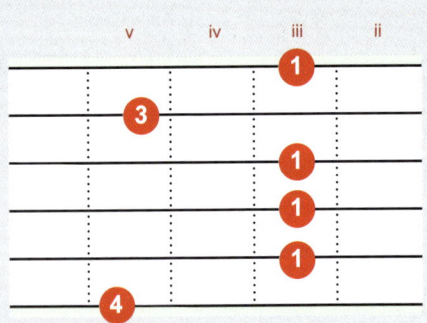

MINOR PENTATONIC SCALE

The minor pentatonic scale is one of the most-used patterns of notes on the guitar—particularly on the electric guitar, as it is a crucial basic building block for constructing a guitar solo in a given key.

"Penta" means five, but we are going to add a sixth note to take you a full octave from your starting note. That sixth note will also be the first note of your next pentatonic scale in that same key, as the aim here is to show you how to string these five note sequences together in a daisy chain all the way up the neck of the guitar—and back.

The fingering for the five notes will be 1-3-1-3-1 (first finger, third finger, etc.). For the sixth note, use finger 1 again and your hand will be in the perfect position to continue your next octave of pentatonic scale.

You have one absolutely crucial lesson to learn before we begin. Because **the minor pentatonic does not begin with the root note of the scale**. If we're doing it in D minor, for instance, we're not going to start with a D. To find the starting note for our scale, we need to turn first to the Major scale and locate the fourth note. That is our starting note.

So, in D, we look first at the D Major scale. First a D—the root note, or tonic. Then an E, then an F#. Now we arrive at the fourth note—a G. So the starting note for our D minor pentatonic scale is a G. We have a choice of Gs in a few different sites on our guitar fretboard, but we're going to find the lowest one, the third fret on the bottom E string.

D MINOR PENTATONIC SCALE

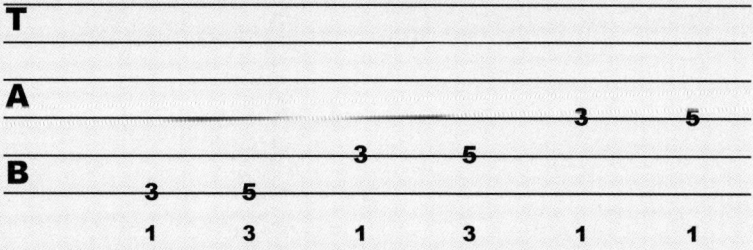

There you have it: a five-note scale. The sixth note, played with your first finger, is actually the first note of your next D minor pentatonic scale, one octave above the one you just played.

So now we're going to string the two together. This is known as a double pentatonic.

LEVEL FIVE

D MINOR DOUBLE PENTATONIC SCALE

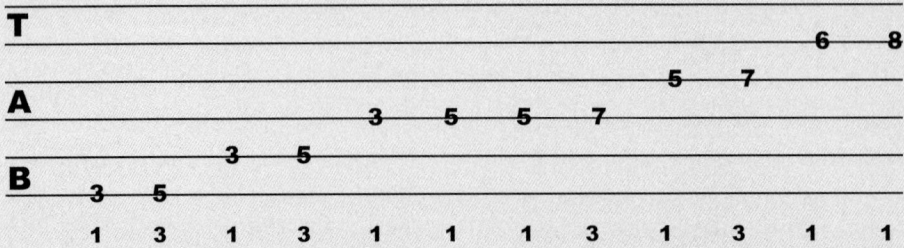

Your last two notes are in a different position, but this is only an adjustment we have to make to allow for the different tuning of the B string. Essentially, you are just repeating the octave below pentatonic scale, but with this minor (sorry!) necessary adjustment. Play a chord of D minor, then play this double pentatonic scale. You'll hear how this could be your springboard to building a solo in that key.

Let's try the same thing in the key of E. Remember, it won't be starting with an E! The first four notes of an E Major scale go E, F#, G#, then A, so A is our starting note. The root note E will be your fourth note. Whatever key you're in, that's where the root note will always sit on the grid—in P4.

E MINOR DOUBLE PENTATONIC SCALE

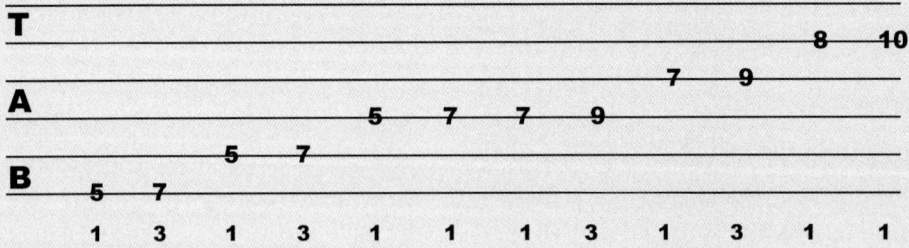

Again, make the adjustment to accommodate the tuning of the B string. But you begin to see how repeatable this five-note pattern is all over the fretboard, so long as you follow the first basic rule to discover your starting note by identifying the fourth note in the Major scale of the key you're in.

Can you see from where you ended up here (on B10)—you're on the first note of the next pentatonic scale? B10, B12, E10, E12—then you run out of road.

A MINOR DOUBLE PENTATONIC SCALE

The first four notes of an A Major scale are A, B, C#, and D, so D will be our starting note (with root note A sitting fourth).

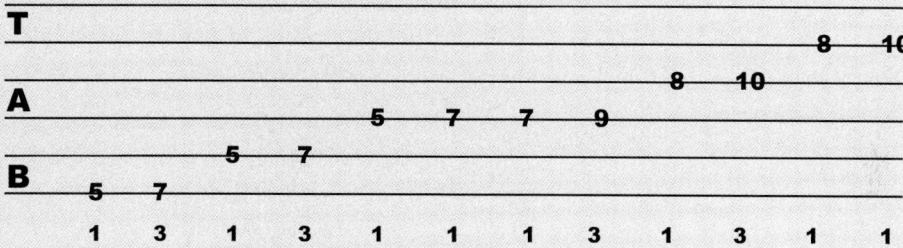

- Try doing it forward, then backward, from top note to bottom.
- Try doing it without repeating note six, at the beginning of the next octave of your scale, so the two octaves flow seamlessly.
- Try applying it to other keys.
- Get used to it—it's the way forward!

LEVEL FIVE

THE BLUES

In the beginning there was the blues—yes, all modern music did grow out of it. So it is for the guitarist. Trust me, it all begins with the blues. Stickers at the ready—should you need them.

BLUES SCALE

The minor pentatonic will get you so far as a lead guitarist, but the blues scale will get you further, and it's a natural development from what you have just learned. This is almost the same scale—just a bit groovier.

Let's leap straight in with a double blues scale, in G. Take care to observe the correct finger positions running along the bottom of the tab.

Once you're used to it, try it up and down. As soon as you hit the top note on E3, it becomes the first note of your descent.

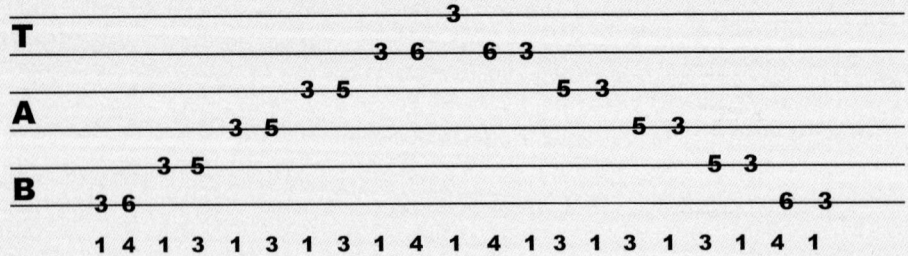

BLUES SCALE 2

Just when you find you've mastered one blues scale in G, along comes another one!

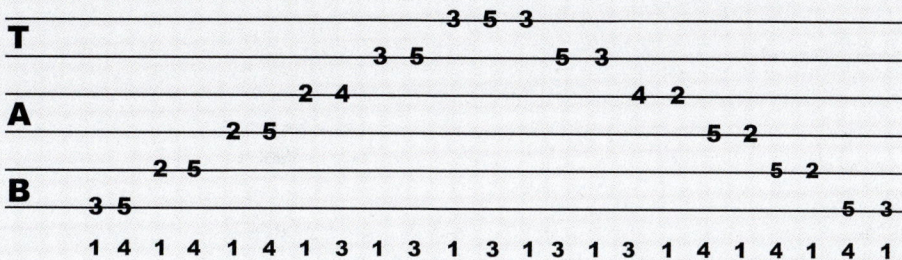

LEAD GUITAR TECHNIQUES
AND TAB SYMBOLS

When reading tabs, you will come across symbols representing the various guitar techniques lead players use to add expression and make single-note work really sing. Here are some techniques and how to play them:

Hammer-on: Pluck a first note and bring a finger down hard on a second note (in front of it on the same string), so that it sounds without you plucking the string.

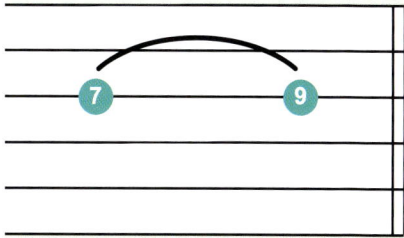

LEVEL FIVE

Pull-off: Play a first note with your second finger beneath it on the same string on the second note. Remove your first note finger the moment you play it, allowing the second note to sound.

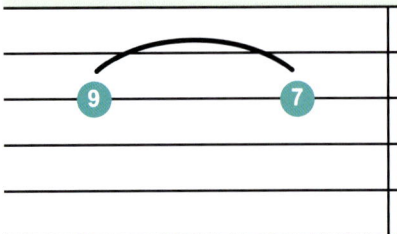

Bend: Force the string upward (toward the ceiling) until you have raised the pitch of the note by a semitone.

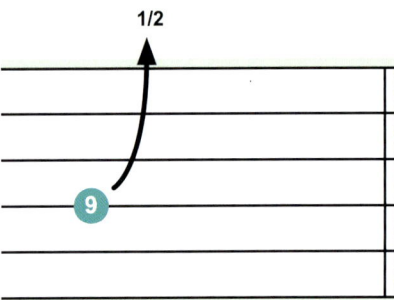

Full bend: force the string upward (toward the ceiling) until you have raised the pitch of the note by a full tone. Be brave—the string won't snap!

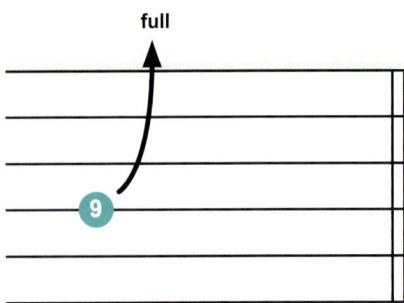

Release bend: Bend your note upward . When it's in position at maximum tension, pluck the note and gradually bring the string back down to its normal position.

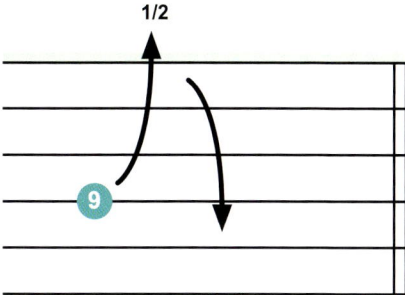

Slide up: Pluck your note, then slide your finger up to the next note on the same string without re-plucking.

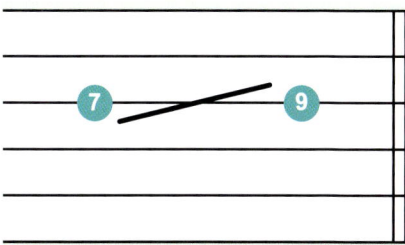

Slide down: Pluck your note, then slide your finger down to the next note on the same string, without re-plucking.

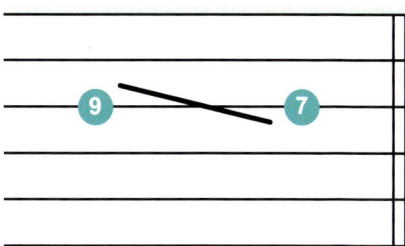

LEVEL FIVE

Palm mute: You don't always want your note or chord to ring. You can produce a great chug-chug bit of rock 'n' roll tension by playing with the heel of your thumb (on your strumming hand) laying across the relevant string or strings, close to the bridge, just allowing a short, muted sound to escape. In this way, you can control exactly how much of the note or chord sounds, and for how long. It's a great way to enhance the rhythm.

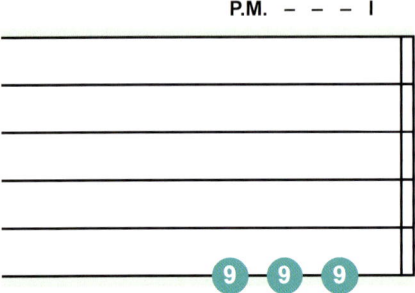

Tapping: A scorching lead solo technique. Instead of plucking the sequence of notes down by the bridge, your picking hand "taps out" the notes high up on the fingerboard.

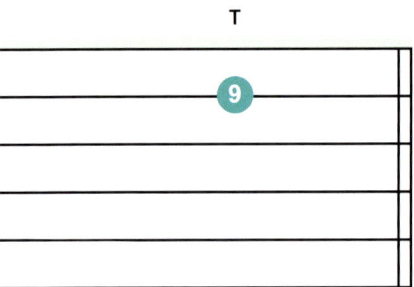

Strumming upstroke:

Strumming downstroke:

When you strum, let yourself go—express yourself. Tutorials will never adequately convey the ever-changing rhythms within a contemporary song. Like allowing yourself to dance, you must unleash your strumming hand to respond to the beat. It's an instinctive thing.

TWELVE-BAR **BLUES**

We know that making a Major chord out of the first note of the Major scale (also known as the tonic), the fourth note (also known as the subdominant), and the fifth note (also known as the dominant) gives us the three "right" chords in that key. It was referred to earlier in this book as "the three-chord trick." These are the only three chords you need to play a twelve-bar blues.

Here's the sequence:

1 - 1 - 1 - 1 - 4 - 4 - 1 - 1 - 5 - 4 - 1 - 5

So, if we're in the key of E, for instance, that translates into four bars of E, two bars of A (because A is the fourth note in the E Major scale), two bars of E, one bar of B (because B is the fifth note of the E Major scale), one bar of A, one bar of E, and finally, one bar of B. Twelve bars in all.

If you were to deliver those three Major chords as (dominant) 7ths, it would sound bluesier!

Play this in swing time, using an eighth beat strum:

1	AND	2	AND	3	AND	4	AND	1	AND	2	AND	3	AND	4	AND
E⁷							-	E⁷							

1	AND	2	AND	3	AND	4	AND	1	AND	2	AND	3	AND	4	AND
E⁷							-	E⁷							

1	AND	2	AND	3	AND	4	AND	1	AND	2	AND	3	AND	4	AND
A⁷							-	A⁷							

1	AND	2	AND	3	AND	4	AND	1	AND	2	AND	3	AND	4	AND
E⁷							-	E⁷							

1	AND	2	AND	3	AND	4	AND	1	AND	2	AND	3	AND	4	AND
B⁷							-	A							

1	AND	2	AND	3	AND	4	AND	1	AND	2	AND	3	AND	4	AND
E							-	B⁷							

LEVEL FIVE

The only variation on this you are likely to meet is a switch to the "fourth note" chord on bar 2:

1 - 4 - 1 - 1 - 4 - 4 - 1 - 1 - 5 - 4 - 1 - 5

Let's now develop this a stage further. With your little finger, add the note two frets above your chord on the A string, on the 2 and the 4.

When you're playing **E⁷**, finger 4 is extending to A⁴—A string fret 4: a C#. Like this:

E⁷

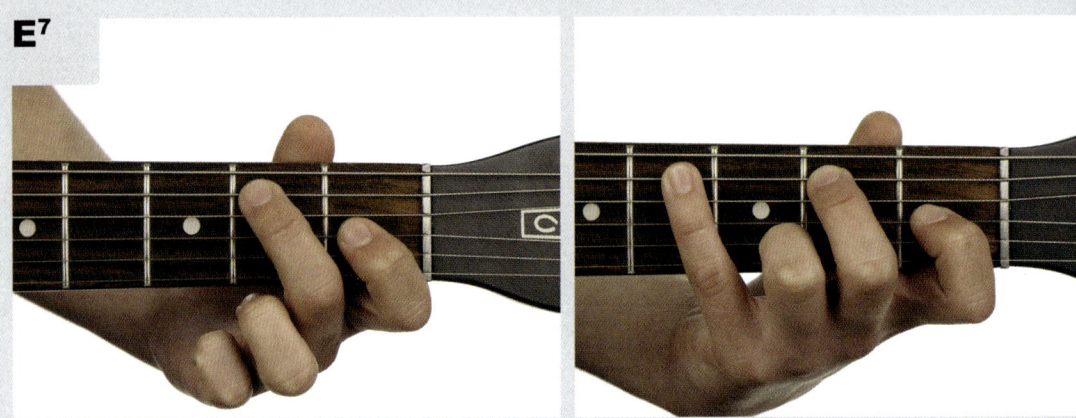

When you're playing **A⁷**, you are going to use the barre version of the chord, finger 1 barring across the fifth fret and finger 4 extending to A⁹ every couple of strums, like this:

A⁷

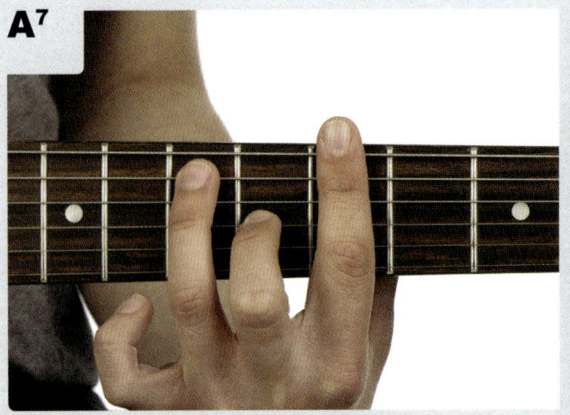

Same thing with **B⁷**—two frets higher, finger 1 barring across the seventh fret and finger 4 extending to A¹¹ every couple of strums, like this:

B⁷

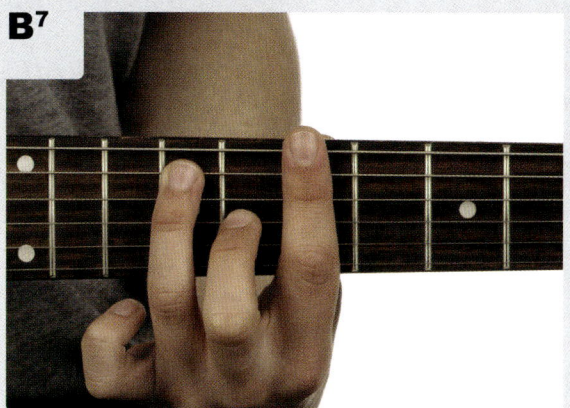

Here's the sequence, with an asterisk added to the chord whenever you need to play it with your little finger on that A string note. (Technically, it's then a 7th with an added 6th—let's just call the chords E*, A*, and B*.)

1 AND	2 AND	3 AND	4 AND		1 AND	2 AND	3 AND	4 AND
E^7	E^{7*}	E^7	E^{7*}	-	A^7	A^{7*}	A^7	A^{7*}

1 AND	2 AND	3 AND	4 AND		1 AND	2 AND	3 AND	4 AND
E^7	E^{7*}	E^7	E^{7*}	-	E^7	E^{7*}	E^7	E^{7*}

1 AND	2 AND	3 AND	4 AND		1 AND	2 AND	3 AND	4 AND
A^7	A^{7*}	A^7	A^{7*}	-	A^7	A^{7*}	A^7	A^{7*}

1 AND	2 AND	3 AND	4 AND		1 AND	2 AND	3 AND	4 AND
E^7	E^{7*}	E^7	E^{7*}	-	E^7	E^{7*}	E^7	E^{7*}

1 AND	2 AND	3 AND	4 AND		1 AND	2 AND	3 AND	4 AND
B^7	B^{7*}	B^7	B^{7*}	-	A^7	A^{7*}	A^7	A^{7*}

1 AND	2 AND	3 AND	4 AND		1 AND	2 AND	3 AND	4 AND
E^7	E^{7*}	E^7	E^{7*}	-	B^7		B^7	

LEVEL FIVE

There are a couple of variations you could throw in, too.

On your B⁷ᵗʰ, you could strum the open version instead of the barre version. On the chord of A, try playing the open version like this: finger 1 across fret 2, covering the three fretted strings that you usually use fingers 1, 2, and 3 to cover:

This leaves fingers 2 and 3 free to embellish the chord with this bluesy sequence of notes (numbers stacked one on top of the other indicates a chord):

```
         1   AND   2   AND   3   AND   4   AND
T ───────────────────────────────────────────────
         2    2              2    2         2
         2    2              2    2    4    2
A        2    2    3    4
  ───────────────────────────────────────────────
B ───────────────────────────────────────────────

         1    1    2    3    1    1    3    1
```

On bar 11 of the twelve-bar sequence, strike the chord of E⁷ on beat 1, then fingerpick this little "run down" with thumb and forefinger, instead of continuing to strum the chord:

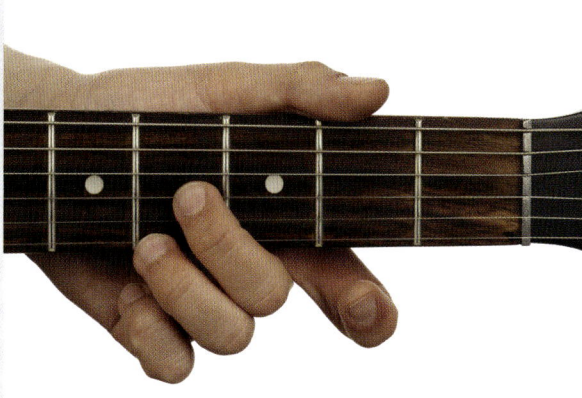

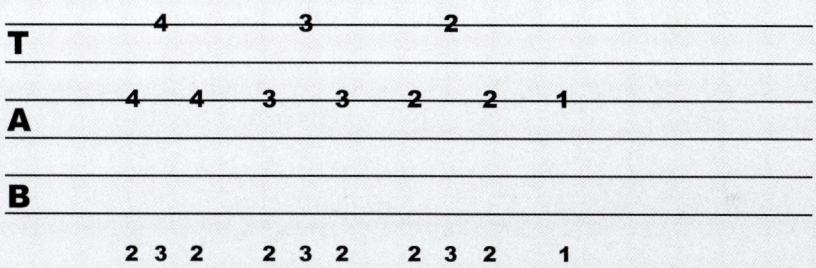

There are countless examples of twelve-bar blues in popular music. This can be at all different speeds, in all different keys. Get comfortably fluent with the twelve-bar blues, for it is a universal language and the perfect starting point for jamming with your friends.

LEVEL FIVE

CIRCLE OF **FIFTHS**

Remember Dan Brown's *The Da Vinci Code*? Professor Robert Langdon, fictional professor of symbology would have loved this! Nothing is more perfectly formed than a circle. And this mystical wheel—the circle of fifths—is so symmetrically balanced in every way, it is a thing of beauty.

We have spoken in this book about scales, firsts, fourths, and fifths, Major chords, relative minors—it's all here, at a glance; it holds all the answers.

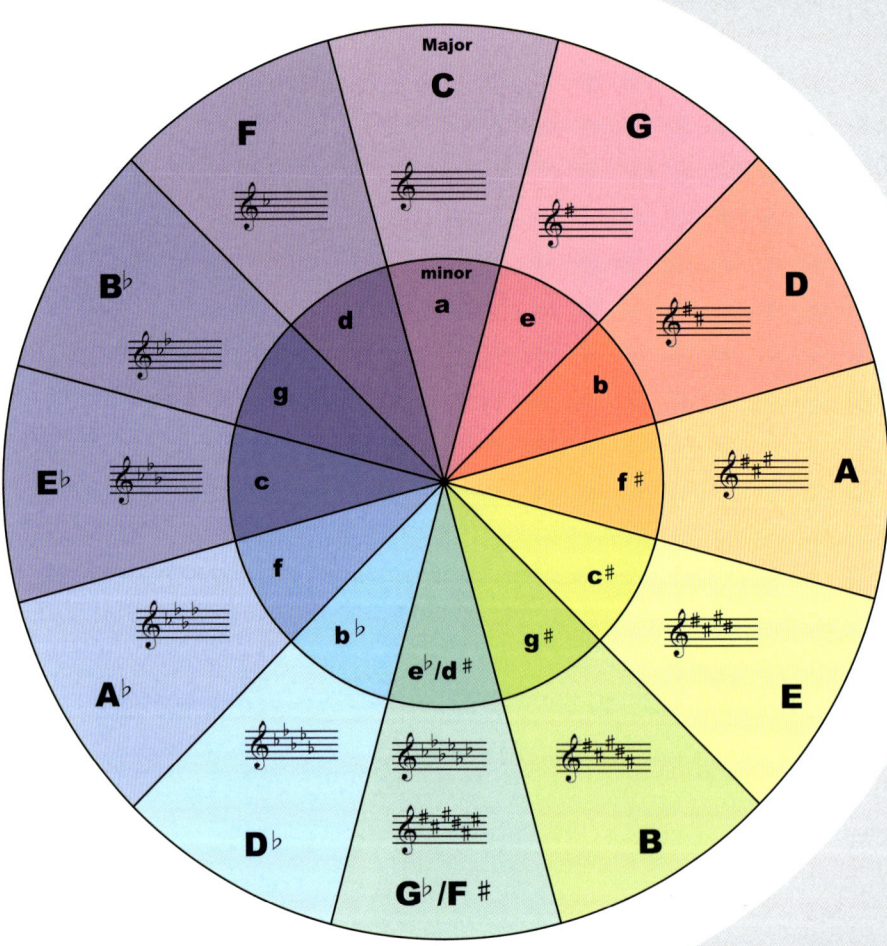

Reading it clockwise from the C, all the capital letters around the outside are five notes of the scale apart. Fifths. Hence the title. Reading it counterclockwise from the C, all the capital letters around the outside are four notes of the scale apart. Fourths. Go back to the C. We can tell at a glance the two chords that go with it, because the fourth is on its left and the fifth is on its right. And the same is true for every single scale around the outside. G? The fourth is a C (its neighbor on the left), the fifth is a D (its neighbor on the right). The two chords that go with D, where D is the root? G and A. The two chords that go with A, where A is the root? D and E. And so on.

The inner circle contains lowercase letters. These are all minors—relative minors. Each letter falls within a segment. Go back to the C. The letter that falls within its slice of the cake is an "a." It tells us that C's relative minor is an A minor. G's relative minor is an E minor, and so on.

The scales we play have a mystifying number of sharps and flats. We remember that C blessedly doesn't have any (played on the piano it is all the white notes), but how do we remember how many the rest of them have? Just refer to the circle of fifths to find the answer. Reading clockwise from the C, they are arranged in such a way that a sharp is added to each scale as we go around, until round about C#, where the number of sharps becomes too heavy to bear and they turn into flats, decreasing all the way around until we are back at C.

There are other symmetrical features of this wheel (keys directly opposite one another, for instance, are all six semitones apart)—but let's keep it simple. The circle is here to serve and inform our immediate requirements:

- To show us at a glance the number of sharps or flats in every key.
- To tell us the first, fourth, and fifth in any key, so that we can turn them into three Major chords and jam along with them.
- To give us their three relative minors, so that we now have six great chords in every key—three Major, three minor—with which to write millions of songs!

You've got the circle of fifths, you've got the blues . . .

YOU'RE A MUSE!

LEVEL FIVE

RIFF REWARD (MUSE)

Congratulations, you've earned a Riff Reward!

When Guns N' Roses put out "Sweet Child O' Mine," they were supporting Aerosmith on a US tour. Aerosmith, who had been through all the trials and tribulations of rock 'n' roll madness, put a protective big-brotherly arm around them.

As for "Sweet Child," it was Guns N' Roses' breakthrough single. By the end of the tour they were bigger than Aerosmith. But guitarist Slash (who invented it) thought the riff "silly" and wanted nothing to do with it. Didn't do him any harm, though! And it has stood the test of time—now everyone wants to play it.

Recreate something similar—the same phrase, twice in succession. Pay careful attention to the picking-hand finger instruction running along the bottom of the tab. Twice in this short sequence (indicated by *), fretting-hand notes are played by a finger already pressed down on a string, by "rocking" that finger flat across the strings from the note it is already holding down. Why? Because it's fast, and it helps you maintain the hand shape you need for this repetitive eight-note pattern.

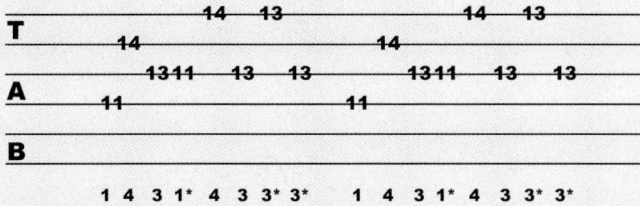

Next two bars, all you need do is change the first note. Keep everything else the same:

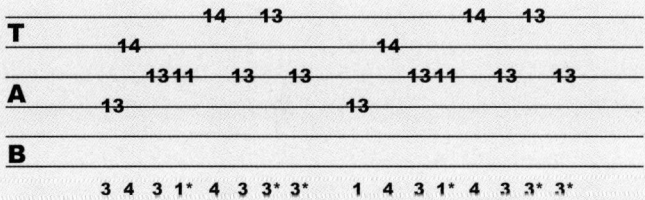

It's an eight-bar sequence, with just the first note changing each time. Here are your next two bars:

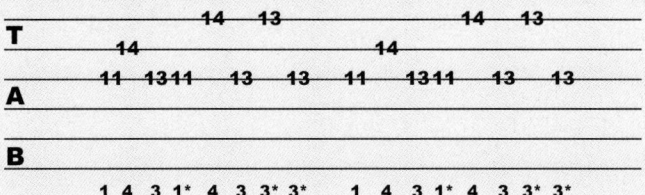

For the last two bars, simply repeat the first two, which started with finger 1 on D^{11}.

Left: Matt Bellamy of Muse

GLOSSARY

acoustic guitar—a guitar that produces sound through the vibration of the strings when they are played; the sound waves from the strings resonate through the guitar's body.

amp/amplifier—an electronic device used to increase the volume of the sound produced by electric guitars.

arpeggiate—plucking individual notes of a chord, in a sequence.

barre chord—a type of chord where your first finger forms a bar across all the strings.

beat—unit of musical rhythm.

bend—pushing or pulling a string upward to raise the pitch of a note.

blues—a type of music of African-American folk origin, usually in a twelve-bar sequence.

bridge—the part of a guitar that holds the strings in place.

CAGED—an acronym for a chord system where a barre chord set-up consists of five shapes, taking you up and down the neck in distinct zones, using the open Major chords of C, A, G, E, and D.

capo—a clamp that you attach to the neck of your guitar to raise the pitch of all the strings equally and simultaneously.

chord—a group of notes played together.

crotchet—a note where four beats is a quarter of a bar.

diminished—a chord with its intervals as the first, flat third, and flat fifth of the Major scale.

dominant—a type of chord that is used to expand or make another chord sound like the home key.

downstroke—a downward strum across the strings, toward the floor.

electric guitar—a guitar that has built-in pick-ups that convert the vibration of the strings into electrical signals for amplification.

fingerboard—a flat strip on the neck of a guitar, against which the strings are pressed to shorten the vibrating length and produce higher pitched notes. (Also called a fretboard.)

fingerpick—using fingernails or fingertips to pluck the strings of a guitar.

flat—a symbol that indicates a note is to be diminished by one semitone.

fret—the space between fret bars.

fret bar—one of a sequence of ridges on the fingerboard of a guitar.

fretboard—a flat strip on the neck of a guitar, against which the strings are pressed to shorten the vibrating length and produce higher pitched notes. (Also called a fingerboard.)

guitar tuner—a device that can help you tune your guitar.

hammer-on—a guitar technique of hammering down hard on a string that's already ringing. (The opposite of a pull-off.)

headstock—the part of a guitar attached to the top of the neck.

key—a group of notes based on and named after a particular note and comprising a scale.

machine head—attachments to the headstock of a guitar; these adjust the tension of the strings, allowing you to retune the strings.

Major chord—a chord with its intervals at the first, third, and fifth notes of the Major scale.

minor chord—a chord with its intervals as the first, flat third, and fifth notes of the Major scale.

neck—the part of a guitar that holds the frets and the strings, upon which chords are played.

note—a single tone of a fixed pitch.

nut—the part of a guitar that separates the fretboard from the headstock, keeping the strings in their correct positions.

octave—a series of eight notes from the root note.

palm mute—a guitar technique using the edge of the palm to control exactly how much of the note or chord sounds and for how long.

peg-winder—a device that makes it quicker and easier to restring your guitar, as it allows you to unwind the pegs faster than by hand.

pentatonic scale—a scale of five notes.

pick—a small triangular object used for strumming or plucking the strings. (Also called a plectrum.)

pitch—the frequency of a note.

plectrum—a small triangular object used for strumming or plucking the strings. (Also called a pick.)

portamento—an uninterrupted slide from one note to another.

powerchord—technically not a chord, but contains only the root and fifth notes, and used for a loud sound.

pull-off—a new note made by pulling your finger off an already ringing note to a lower fretted or open note. (The opposite of a hammer-on.)

quaver—an eighth of a bar in 4/4 time.

root—the first note of a scale or chord. (Also called a tonic.)

saddle—the raised area on a guitar's bridge upon which the strings sit.

scale—a series of notes in ascending or descending order of pitch that lie within an octave.

semitone—the interval between two adjacent notes in a twelve-tone scale. (Also called a half-step.)

sharp—a symbol to indicate a note is to be raised by one semitone.

slide—a technique of sliding notes or chord shapes up the fretboard.

string—a piece of wire or nylon attached to a guitar, which produces musical notes via vibrations when played.

string peg—a device used to peg the end of a string into the bridge of a guitar.

strum—playing more than one string in the same movement up or down.

sus/suspended—a dominant chord where the third is replaced by the fourth, a half step higher.

syncopated strumming—a strumming technique that leaves out actual beats and plays divisions or subdivisions around them; used to create a more diverse rhythm.

tab/tablature—a system of notation consisting of six horizontal lines to represent the strings, and numbers that indicate which fret to play.

tone—a sound characterized by its pitch, quality, and strength.

tonic—the first note of a scale or chord. (Also called a root.)

tremolo arm—a device attached to an electric guitar that bends the strings, creating a unique sound. (Also called a whammy bar.)

upstroke—an upward stroke across the strings, toward the ceiling.

whammy bar—a device attached to an electric guitar that bends the strings, creating a unique sound. (Also called a tremolo arm.)

INDEX

4ths, suspended 116–18
6ths
  Major 135–41
  minor 143–9
7ths
  dominant 78–91
  major 92–100
  minor 100–16
9ths
  dominant 150–1
  minor 152–8

A
A dominant 7th 35, 80–1
A Major 34
  barre chord 65
  CAGED chords 119–22
  Major 6th 135
  Major 7th 38, 92–3
  pentatonic scale 124
  relative minor 72
  scale 72
A minor 21, 65, 71, 143
  double pentatonic scale 160
  minor 6th 144
  minor 7th 24, 101–2
  minor 9th 152
A powerchord 60
A sharp powerchord 57
A sus 4th 117
acoustic guitar 12
arpeggiating 51–2
augmented chords 134

B
B dominant 7th 38, 90–1
B Major 67
  Major 6th 136
  Major 7th 93–4
B minor 39, 69, 70, 71, 151
  minor 6th 145
  minor 7th 103–4
  minor 9th 153
barre chords 64
  CAGED chords 119–22

bend 164
Blues
  scale 162–3
  twelve-bar 167–71
bridge 12

C
C dominant 7th 86–7
C dominant 9th 150
C Major 25
  CAGED chords 119–22
  Major 6th 137
  Major 7th 25, 94–5
  relative minor 71
  scale 41
C minor 40, 69–70, 143
  minor 6th 146
  minor 7th 105–6
  minor 9th 154
C powerchord 63
C sharp powerchord 58
  CAGED chords 119–22
capo 22
cartoon chords 134
chord families 78
circle of fifths 172–3

D
D dominant 7th 37, 82–3
D Major 36, 66
  CAGED chords 119–22
  Major 6th 138
  Major 7th 96–7
  relative minor 71, 72
  scale 72
D minor 36, 66
  double pentatonic scale 160
  minor 6th 147
  minor 7th 107–9
  minor 9th 155
  pentatonic scale 159
D powerchord 61
D sus 4th 117
diminished chords 134
dominant 7ths 78–89

E
E dominant 7th 24, 78–9
E dominant 9th 150–1
E Major 22
  CAGED chords 119–22
  Major 6th 139
  Major 7th 97–8
  relative minor 73
  scale 73
E minor 23, 71
  double pentatonic scale 160
  minor 6th 148
  minor 7th 110–12
  minor 9th 156
E sus 4th 118
eighth beats 34
electric guitar 13

F
F dominant 7th 88–9
F Major 7th 29
F Major
  barre chord 67
  Major 6th 26, 140
  Major 7th 99–100
F minor 68
  minor 7th 113–14
  minor 9th 157
fifths 172–3
finger names 10
fingerboard 12
fingerboard diagrams 10
fingernails 14
fingerpicking 130–3
flats 11
Foo 48–75
four in the bar 6/8 time 50–2
fretboard 14
frets 12, 15
  bars 12, 15
  fingerboard diagrams 10
  guitar tab 41
  markers 15
fretting hand 14, 16
full bend 164

G

G dominant 7th 84–5
G Major 43
  barre chord 68
  Blues scale 162–3
  CAGED chords 119–22
  Major 6th 26, 141
  Major 7th 27
  pentatonic scale 125
  powerchord 60
  relative minor 71
  scale 71
G minor
  minor 6th 149
  minor 7th 114–16
  minor 9th 158
  natural minor 142–3
G sharp powerchord 57

H

hammer-on 163
headstock 12
holding a guitar 9
holding a pick 9

I

improvisation 11, 42

J

jack input 13

L

left-handers 8, 10

M

machine heads 12
Major chords 71

N

natural minor 142–3
neck 12
nut 12, 15

P

palm mute 16, 166
peg-winder 28
pentatonic scale 124–5
  minor 159
  minor double 160–1
pick 9
pickup 13
plucking 51–2
portmento 13
powerchords 56
  A 60
  A sharp 57
  C 63
  C sharp 58
  D 61
  G 60
  G sharp 57
pull-off 164
pushed chord 54

Q

quarter beats 20

R

relative minor chords 71–3
release bend 165
right chords 71–3, 167
root note 56
rosette 12

S

saddle 12
scales
  Blues 162–3
  C Major 41
  circle of fifths 172–3
  D Major 72
  dominant 167
  G Major 71
  minor pentatonic 159–61
  modal 47
  natural minor 142–3
  pentatonic 124–5
  subdominant 167
  three-chord trick 42, 71, 167
  tonic 167
scratchboard 12
sharps 11
slide down 165
slide up 165
sound hole 12
strings 14
  changing 28
  fingerboard diagrams 10
  guitar tab 41
strumming 16
  6/8 time 54
  downstroke symbol 166
  syncopated 53
  three in a bar 35
  upstroke symbol 166
strumming hand 14, 16
suspended 4ths 116–18
syncopated strumming 53

T

tab, reading 41
tapping 166
three-chord trick 42, 71, 167
time
  4/4 eighth beats 34
  4/4 quarter beats 20
  6/8 50–2
tone control knobs 13
tonic 167
tuner 28, 30
tuning 30

W

whammy bar 13

Acknowledgments

www.rokskool.co.uk

Rok Skool Sussex gave me the perfect platform for this book. I credit every guitar student of every age and ability who has sat in front of me these past ten years, and every band I have musically mentored within the Rok Skool environment. Each in their own way showed me what they needed to learn and helped streamline my own method of communication and delivery.

My mission has always been to get people playing by ear as quickly as possible. Rok Skool allowed me to organically develop, then sharpen and hone, the musical approach and systems that I have set down in *Guitar Chords—A Fretboard Sticker Book*.

Hereward Kaye

www.herewardkaye.co.uk

Quintet would like to thank musical consultant Kieran Matthews, from Brighton-based band Just Like Fruit.

Credits

Alamy: Trinity Mirror/Mirrorpix 18, 76; Justin Moir 44; AF archive 46; Ashly Covington 48; TNT Magazine 55; MediaPunch Inc 59; Pictorial Press Ltd 61, 109; bill belknap 62; Joe Bird 74; Everynight Images 127; Roberto Finizio 128

Getty: Fin Costello 32; Kevin Winter 45; Gijsbert Hanekroot 123; Brian Rasic/WireImage 174

Neal Grundy (photographer), Rory Indiana Kaye (model): 2, 5, 9, 16, 21, 22–30, 34–43, 56–8, 60-1, 63–70, 78–121, 134–41, 144–50, 152–58, 168–71

+SUBTRACT: 12, 13, 17, 28

Hereward Kaye: 6l

Steve Robards: 6r

Front cover: William Iven: https://pixabay.com/en/users/FirmBee-663163/

While every effort has been made to credit photographers, Quintet Publishing would like to apologize should there have been any omissions or errors, and would be pleased to make the appropriate correction for future editions of the book.

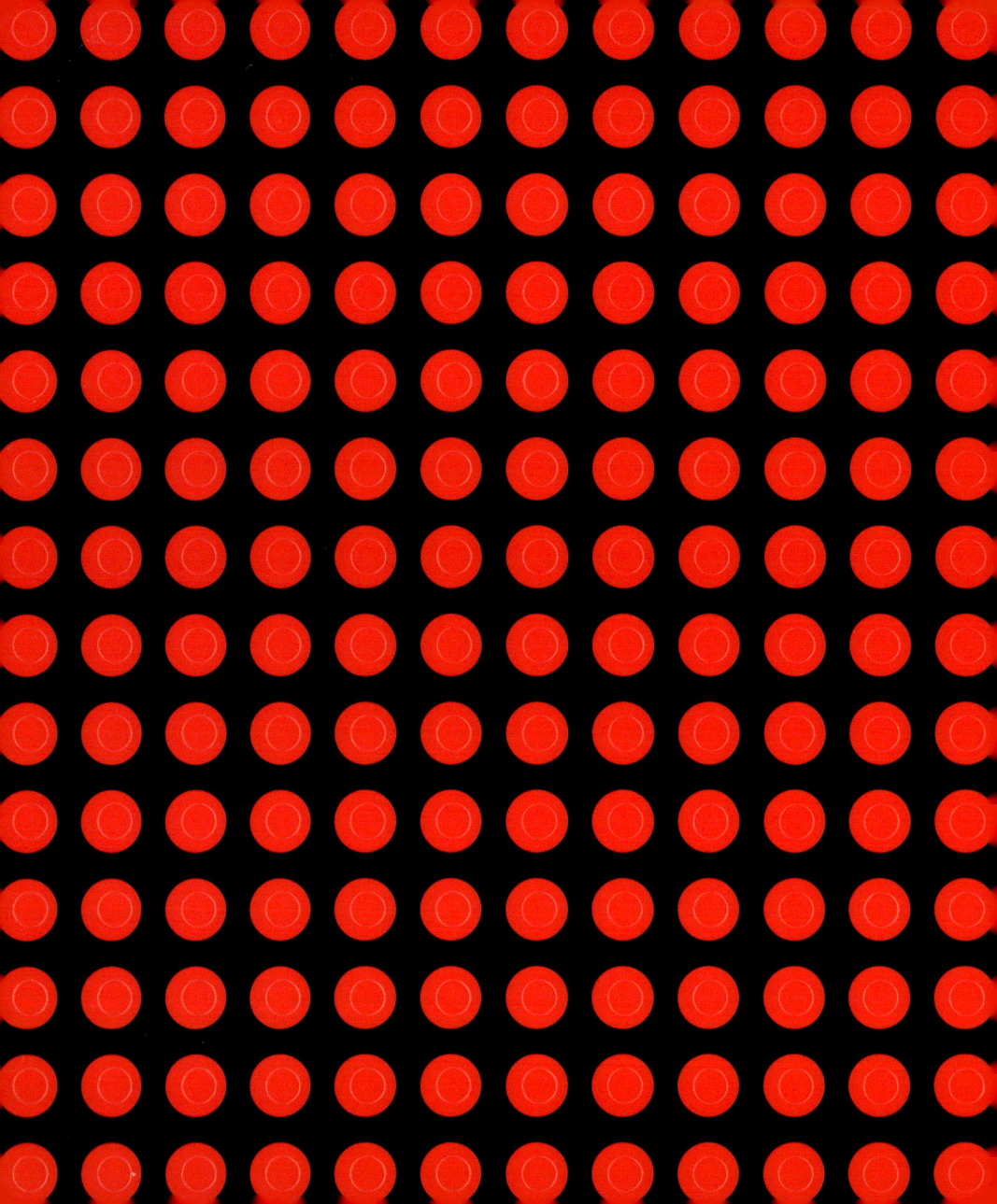

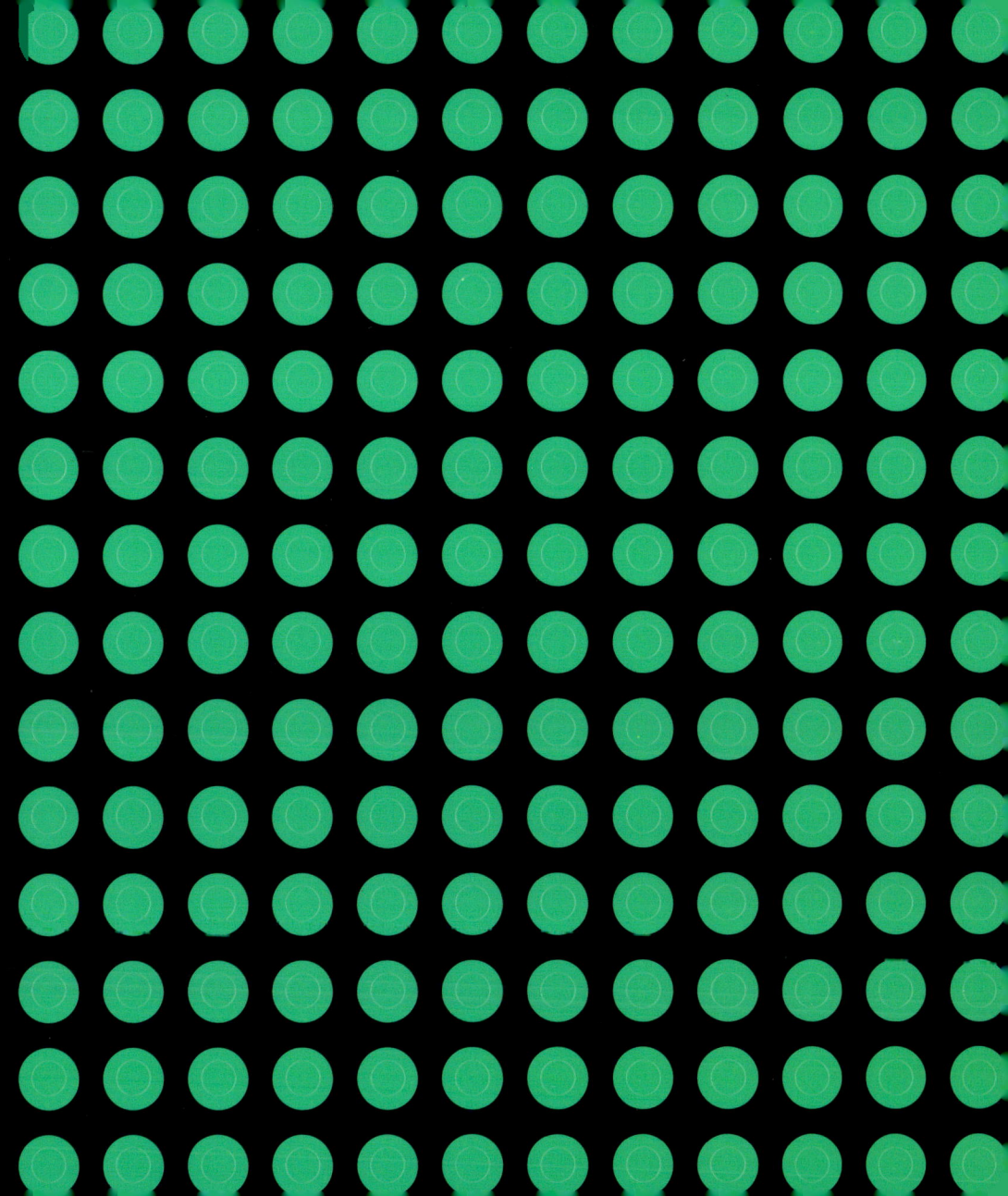

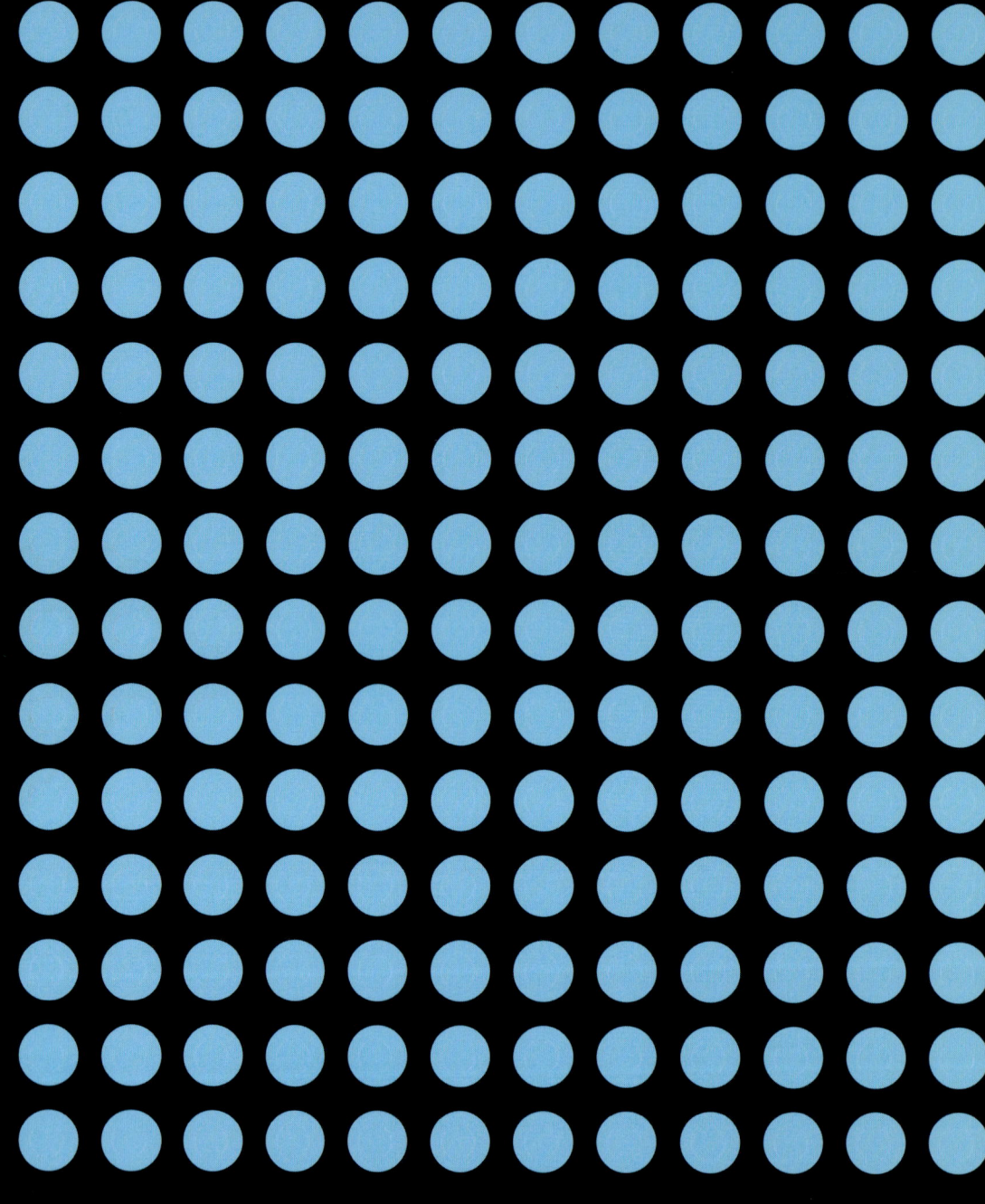

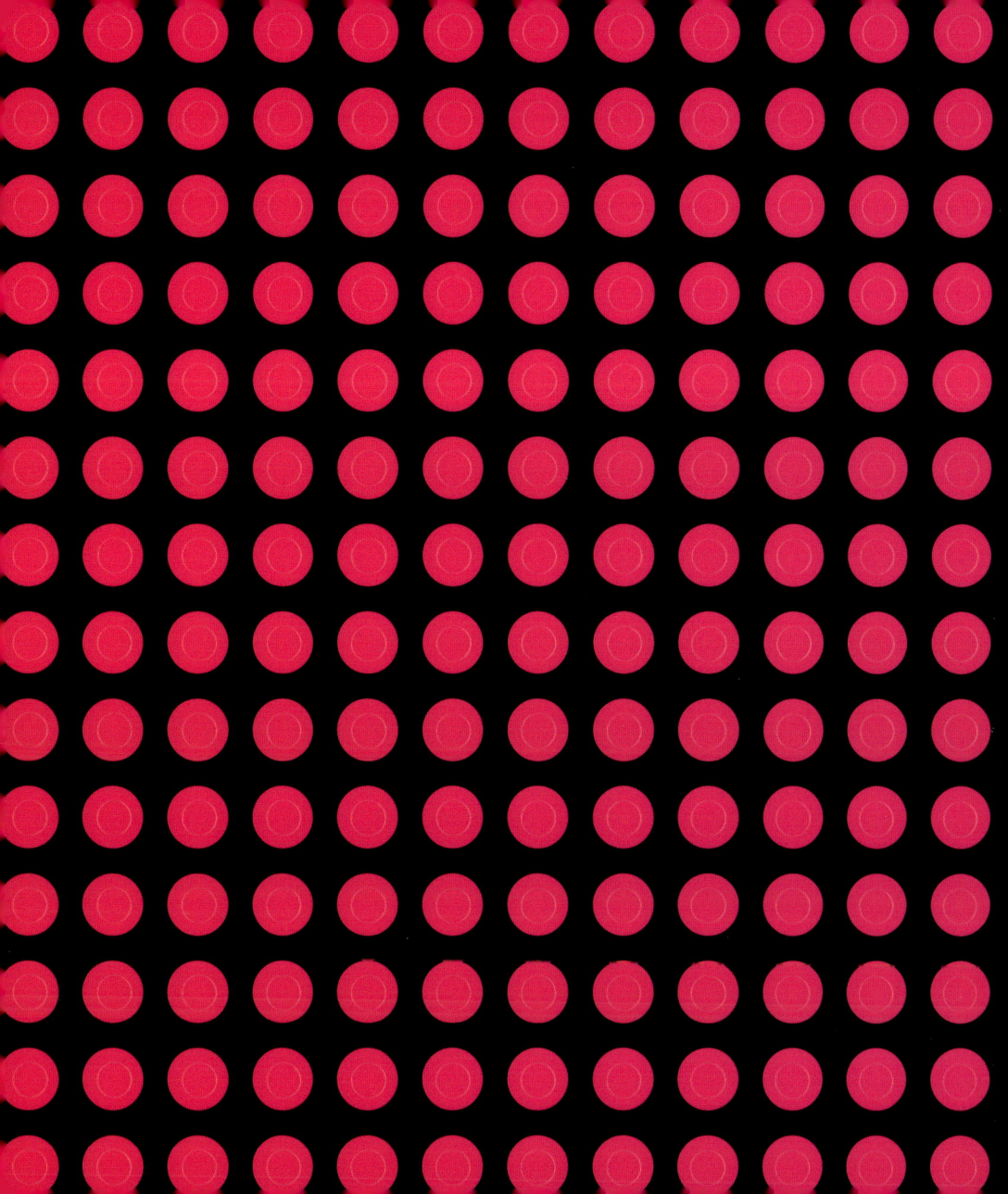